THE Armchair

DETECTIVE #1

THE Armchair DETECTIVE #1

KEN WEBER

Stoddart

Published in 2000 by Stoddart Publishing Co. Limited
34 Lesmill Road, Toronto, Canada M3B 2T6
180 Varick Street, 9th Floor, New York, New York 10014

Distributed in Canada by:
General Distribution Services Ltd.
325 Humber College Blvd., Toronto, Ontario M9W 7C3
Tel. (416) 213-1919   Fax (416) 213-1917
Email cservice@genpub.com

Distributed in the United States by:
General Distribution Services Inc.
PMB 128, 4500 Witmer Industrial Estates,
Niagara Falls, New York 14305-1386
Toll-free Tel.1-800-805-1083   Toll-free Fax 1-800-481-6207
Email gdsinc@genpub.com

04   03   02   01   00   1   2   3   4   5

Canadian Cataloguing in Publication Data

Weber, K.J. (Kenneth Jerome), 1940–
The armchair detective #1
ISBN 0-7737-6142-X

1. Detective and mystery stories, Canadian (English).*
2. Literary recreations.   3. Puzzles. I. Title.
GV1507.D4W416   2000   793.73   C00-931294-3

U.S. Cataloging-in-Publication Data
(Library of Congress Standards)

Weber, Ken
The armchair detective #1 / Ken Weber.
[144]p. : cm. (Armchair Detective Guide)
Summary: In 40 mystery stories, the reader is the detective and is challenged to find the hidden clues and solve the mystery.
ISBN 0-7737-6142-X (pbk.)
1. Detective and mystery stories.   2. Literary recreations.
3. Puzzles.   I. Title. II. Series.
813.54 [F] 2000 CIP

Cover design: Kinetics Design & Illustration
Text design and typesetting: Kinetics Design & Illustration
Cover illustration: Sarah Jane English

THE CANADA COUNCIL | LE CONSEIL DES ARTS
FOR THE ARTS | DU CANADA
SINCE 1957 | DEPUIS 1957

We acknowledge for their financial support of our publishing program the Canada Council, the Ontario Arts Council, and the Government of Canada through the Book Publishing Industry Development Program (BPIDP).

Printed and bound in Canada

To Jack Atkin,
who understands that
a little scotch,
a lot of flowers,
great ladies,
and enduring friendship
are all that really matter.

Contents

Acknowledgments

More than forty times now I've bade fond farewell to a completed manuscript. But I'm still completely dazzled when it reappears a few months later as an honest-to-goodness *book*! This time, for *The Armchair Detective #1*, I have my editor-without-equal, Sue Sumeraj, to thank. They're a strange and wonderful bunch, editors. Not only do they take on your book as if it's their own, they maintain enough distance at the same time to lead you back to the garden path when necessary. A difficult job, and Sue's one of the best at it. For this one she even enlisted her husband, Randy. Thanks, Randy, for poking holes where the structure was weak.

Thanks, too, to the people at Stoddart Publishing, especially Don Bastian for his continuing support. A special thanks to designer extraordinaire Daniel Crack and cover artist Sarah Jane English for getting an understanding of the book before going to work on it. And to my son Stephen, who knows just how to teach his dad to make a computer behave. (Not easy when you're dealing with a guy who remembers that carbon paper never crashed.)

Without Cecile, my wife, best friend, partner-in-mysteries,

and the single best move I ever made, I wouldn't get anything done. She uncovers more mysteries than I do but is kind enough to let me write them.

Finally, a bow of gratitude to all the readers who delighted in my first series, the Five-Minute Mysteries, and took the time to tell me. I have letters from all over Canada and the U.S., and from Europe and Asia. University presidents have written me, police officers, lawyers, a waitress in St. Louis, and a fisherman in Thailand who is learning English.

And I especially thank the kids who have written. The Five-Minute Mysteries series and now this new one, The Armchair Detective series, are put together with a 'G' rating in mind. It's great to know that anyone in a family can read and enjoy them.

KEN WEBER
MAY 30, 2000

Memorandum

To: ALL MYSTERY BUFFS
From: the author of *The Armchair Detective*

Mystery buffs know there are only two kinds of people in the world, those that love mysteries and, well, that other kind. A tiny majority, the latter, and that's a good thing because they are missing something unique. For only in mysteries can a reader get a charge out of winning *or* losing.

It works like this. Nothing gives mystery buffs more satisfaction than getting ahead in a story and beating the writer to the punch. They get a special charge out of combining logic, analysis, intuition, and insight so that before they turn the last page, they already have the problem solved. Yet — and this is what sets mystery lovers apart — nothing thrills them more than when the mystery defeats them, when they turn the last page and find a surprise waiting, something they'd missed.

In *The Armchair Detective*, mystery lovers will get no less than forty shots at the fun of winning or losing in a set of widely different stories. Every mystery in the book is set up for the reader to solve. At the end of each one there is a question: *Who did . . . ?* or *What did . . . ?* or *It seems the thief made a mistake. How could . . . ?* Like that.

There's great variety. The settings range from city to country, from desert to drawing room, and from forensic lab to barn-yard and mountaintop. There are pickpockets and con artists, frauds and murderers, kidnappers and thieves. You'll encounter regular cops and private cops, medical examiners, lawyers, park rangers, sharpshooters, and soldiers. There's even a butler. (He did it too, but you'll have to figure out what he did!)

There's also variety in the level of challenge. As you flip the pages of *The Armchair Detective*, you'll notice footprints at the beginning of each story. The number of footprints suggest how easy or difficult the mystery is. (Or, perhaps more accurately, how easy or difficult each one seems to me.)

Finally, all the solutions are at the back of the book, so you can either prove you're a winner or, once in a while, get a kick out of losing, without ever leaving your armchair. By the way, to enjoy these mysteries, an armchair isn't really essential. Nor is a fireplace or a glass of sherry. Nor even a magnifying glass. All you really need are your wits and enough patience to enjoy a gentle challenge.

Check the Footprints!

Each file in *The Armchair Dectective* is rated according to its level of challenge for the typical mystery reader. The key is the number of footprints shown next to the title. Three footprints, for example, means it's a fairly easy case to solve. Four footprints tells you the case is just a bit harder. And so on . . .

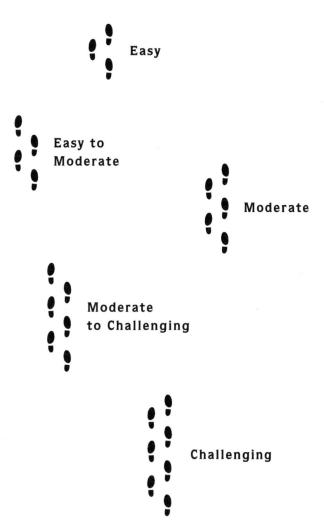

Easy

Easy to
Moderate

Moderate

Moderate
to Challenging

Challenging

Blowing Up the Mackenzie Building

For eighty years the Mackenzie Building had loomed over Pier 12 like a disapproving spinster aunt. Tomorrow that dominance was to come to an end. At strategic points along the eroding, gray foundation and the bottom edge of support walls on every one of the six floors, bright red numbers had been spray-painted with great clarity. They were marker points for the dynamite that would be placed there right after the morning rush hour. By mid-morning, the connections would be completed and double-checked. By noon — in fact, before noon, to minimize the lunch hour gawking crowd — Luther Plantz would do a final walk-through, inspect every single placement, and then press a small red disk that, to him at least, both looked like and really was an official seal.

What it would do tomorrow, that red disk, was seal the fate of the Mackenzie Building and everything in it, for it was really a flat connector that would send electrical instructions in a precise sequence to each placement of dynamite. The building, if things turned out as they always had, would then come tumbling down on itself.

But that was then and this was now, and Luther Plantz was

going through his customary period of pre-blow anxiety. It was more than just nervousness, more than just caution. He always endured a high level of discomfort before a demolition. His employees attributed it to the care he put into every job. Luther, according to those in the business who would know, had never had a failure. For a profession that hung right out there on the edge with every undertaking, that was a pretty significant claim, for there was so much that might go wrong. Effectively demolishing a structure isn't simply a case of combining architecture, engineering, and explosives, Luther always said. You must also cope with politics, sentiment, and sociology. He had never yet taken down an old, established building without encountering opposition from heritage groups, from street people whose shelter was threatened, and, quite understandably, from next-door neighbors at risk.

Curiously, with all those pressures leaping about in his mind as he walked the ground floor of the Mackenzie Building, what bothered him far more was what he perceived to be the attitude of his oldest son beside him. Although in physique and body language, Bruno Plantz was practically a clone of his father, inside he was . . . well, as Luther had said to his wife for the hundredth time just hours before: "He's good. He knows how to blow 'em up. But he doesn't *understand*. It's like . . . It's like he's almost got no *feelings*. I tell him time and again. This isn't just a business; these are buildings that *mean* something. Something to the community, or to people. These buildings have a *soul*. But he doesn't want to know about that!"

And for the hundredth time, his wife had given her stock answer. "He's young. Wait a while."

That dialogue was re-running in Luther's head as he turned on an old iron faucet that stuck out of an interior wall. There was an instant response and clear water gushed out with enough pressure to make both men step back.

"Now see," Luther said, as Bruno rolled his eyes, knowing what was coming. "There's workmanship. That's why every building has something special about it. This place hasn't been used for, what, seven years? Power was cut off years ago. All the machinery emptied out. Nothing in here but pigeons and derelicts all that time and here you have something somebody did so well eighty years ago that, even though there's an idiot down at city hall didn't do his job and cut the water off, the plumbing still works. That's what you gotta respect when we take something down."

Two years of partnership with his father had taught Bruno Plantz to say nothing when the older man was expounding in this way.

"And that tells you something very important. If the plumbers were good, you gotta assume the masons were good, too. That's why we're the doing the single stick test one more time."

Bruno maintained his silence. Deep down he respected his father for a practice that few in the industry bothered with any more: small test explosions to assess the strength of the construction. But at the same time, it stirred up another issue the two had argued over: the best choice of explosives. As though to mirror his son's thoughts, Luther subconsciously rolled the back of his hand along the stick of dynamite he was carrying. The day was becoming progressively hotter and more humid, and sweating dynamite, even a single stick, was dangerous.

"If we'd use C4 or Semtex, the humidity wouldn't be a problem," Bruno couldn't hold back.

"Huh? What . . . ? Yes, yes, I know; you and your plastics." Luther was trying hard not to turn this into a spat. "And you're probably right. But there's no *art* with that stuff. When you take down a building like this, you gotta show some *respect*. Dynamite . . . we've been through this before, son, I know, but with dynamite there's more . . . How do I say this? . . . There's more of you and me against those old guys like that plumber and the masons. There's more *game!*"

The younger man shrugged his shoulders. It was obvious he was not going to change his father's view. "Speaking of 'game,' by the way, I think we should bring the cops along for the walk-through tomorrow morning."

"The cops?"

"Yes, the cops. To clear out a 'spectator.'"

"Here? Inside? The Mackenzie Building's been clear for months! You can see for yourself. No litter, no fires. No filthy bedrolls. No cardboard!"

"Dad." Bruno Plantz could not resist a patronizing tone. "Someone is still using this building."

? *How does Bruno Plantz know that someone has still been using the Mackenzie Building?*

FILE # 2

The Worst Kind of Phone Call

"**M**om, there's been an accident.' That's what she said." Laura Pascal was speaking to Karen Tarata but kept her eyes fixed on the road as they sped along Milldown Parkway. It was 1:00 a.m.

"So when she said she was all right, it didn't register at all." Laura continued. "Not until she told me the third time. You'd think she'd have the sense to *start* a midnight phone call with 'I'm OK' and then tell me. Look at me! I'm still shaking!"

"You sure you don't want me to drive?" Karen asked.

Laura shook her head.

Karen stared out the passenger window for a moment before saying, "At least she called you. If you hadn't come over to tell me, that call from the police would have been my first inkling. Come to think of it, that's just how the policeman started too . . . 'Mrs. Tarata, there's been an accident involving your daughter.' And, you know, even though you'd already told me no one was hurt, I could feel the ice pour into my stomach when he spoke."

The drive continued in silence, both women reflecting on the accident and on their relationships with their teenage daughters. Laura Pascal was tense, anxious. She held the steering wheel firmly with both hands and continued to focus completely on the space of light the headlights of her car opened before them. Karen Tarata was equally upset, but her nature was more secretive and her body language more contained.

Laura was the first to break the silence. "The car, apparently, is a write-off." It was the first time either of the two women had mentioned the vehicle. "It . . . it . . ." Her reluctance to deal with the details was more a factor of her own fears than worry that she might upset Karen. "It rolled twice after going through the guard rail so they must have been going pretty fast. Thank God for seat belts."

"It was the Maleski girl? Cara? Her parents' car, right?" Karen spoke without looking away from the passenger window. "I don't know whether it's the accident that's making me say this, but I've never been entirely sure about her."

Laura nodded at the road. "Going to the dance at Milldown High was her idea, but to be honest, Karen, I don't think our girls needed much persuading. You know . . ." For only a second, she broke her driving concentration and looked sideways at her passenger. Laura wasn't sure whether to continue with her thought. The two women were neighbors, not really friends, but had been drawn together more than once in the past because their daughters "hung out."

"No matter how I try," she carried on, "I can't understand their social pattern, these girls. My Allie, she's seventeen, and, you know, the grad dance last month was the *first* time she went on an actual *date*. You know, where the boy actually knocks on the *door*. Comes to pick her up. And then brings her *home* again!"

There was another silence, then, still looking out the side window, Karen said, "Liberation." There was another pause. "It's the first stage in liberation. The first thing you do when you're set free is act like your oppressors."

Laura turned away from the road again, this time with new interest. Here was a facet of her neighbor that she'd never encountered.

"And because males cluster in groups and take on a group personality, that's what girls do now, too. From what you told me, that's probably what caused this whole thing tonight. Your Allie and that Cara, and Jenine — who was the fourth one? The Lotten girl from one street over? — the spat with that group of boys in the parking lot would never have turned into an incident if they weren't acting as a group. Individuals back down, walk away. Groups fight. Imagine! Girls being asked to leave a dance. There's liberation for you."

Just ahead, the lights of Milldown were visible on the horizon. Laura slowed to obey the new speed limit.

"But Allie told me they left without a fuss," she pointed out. "It was when they were on their way back home to Porterville — they were about halfway she said — that they saw headlights coming up behind them and recognized the boys' car. So — maybe it was Cara's first instinct; who's got judgment at that age? — she speeded up to get away and . . . well . . . you know the rest."

Karen not only turned away from the passenger window, she shifted completely, so that her body was facing Laura. "And you bought that story?" she said.

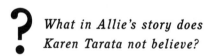

? *What in Allie's story does Karen Tarata not believe?*

FILE # 3

A Courtly Gesture

The two insurance investigators were almost exactly the same age. The same weight and build, too, and when the one with the pencil-line moustache wore his black shoes with the elevator heels — which he did every day — they were the same height. In every other way they were as different as could be. The man with the moustache — his name was Aubrey — was precise, organized, methodical, business-like. On alternate days he wore a brown or a gray suit. With the brown suit he wore a forest green bow-tie; with the gray, the bow-tie was maroon with royal blue dots. The shirt was always white. Everyone at the company, superiors, equals, office staff, called him Mr. Beckwith. No one ever called him Aubrey.

Except for the man walking at his side right now. Jerry Fawcett was the only one. Jerry even called him "Aub" on occasion. But that was Jerry, whose real name was Gerard — but hardly anyone knew that. It wouldn't have mattered anyway. He was a nickname kind of guy. Easygoing with a ready smile, and blessed, it seemed, with both endless patience and a bottomless well of interest in whomever he happened to be with. Women loved him. Men liked him — even Aubrey, who didn't much like anyone.

At the moment, the two were walking away from the house they had just visited, and as usual they were arguing. Not vigorously, but with the low-grade and seemingly constant level of disagreement that characterized their unlikely partnership.

"That was a bit over the top, the kissing the hand thing." Aubrey had a surprisingly rich baritone voice. Most people, at first glance, would have expected something prissy, especially now, for he was annoyed at his partner.

Minutes before, as they stood to leave the house, Jerry had made a sweeping bow to the claimant and, with both his hands, raised one of hers to his lips and kissed it, in an old-world fashion. Although Aubrey would never have admitted it, even to himself, he had been impressed with how natural the gesture had been.

"In fact, way over the top!" Aubrey was warming up to a scolding now. "We're supposed to be *investigating* her, not courting her! If she wins the case she could be into the company for — what — *millions*, maybe?"

Instead of answering, Jerry stopped and put his hand on the other man's shoulder. He was grinning, as though sharing a conspiracy.

"But Aub," he said. "Did you see the expression on her face? And the little blush on the cheeks? Just in front of her ears? She loved it!"

Aubrey suddenly realized that he had stopped automatically when Jerry did. He wrinkled his nose just a tiny bit at the hand on his shoulder, but he didn't step back or try to remove it.

"This woman tells us, Jerry . . ." Aubrey glanced back to the house. He knew his voice carried. "She tells us she's been in that wheelchair since the accident six months ago. Hasn't been able to walk since. She's got that crackpot psychiatrist on her side, but our doctors . . . they can't find anything wrong. Not the orthopedic specialist, not the neurologist. The X-rays don't show a thing. And now, along comes Sir Jerry on his white horse." Aubrey was really winding up now. This time it was Jerry who looked back to the house. "My partner is supposed to be uncovering fraud, but what does he do instead, he . . ."

"Aub — Aubrey! Relax." Jerry put up his other arm, so that now both hands were resting on Aubrey's shoulders. "Trust me. I was investigating. The courtly Sir Jerry has learned that she has not been pushing herself around in that wheelchair for the past six months. No way, OK? She's smooth, that lady. But now that we definitely know she's lying, it shouldn't be too hard to shut the case down."

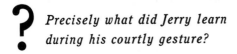 *Precisely what did Jerry learn during his courtly gesture?*

A Dispute on the Ledge

From the bottom of the cliff, toward the north, where the river looped and resumed its flow to the east, the women and children of the tribe could see the two men arguing. The dispute appeared more heated than it really was, for all the two could do was gesture. Neither knew more than a few words of the other's language. One of the men, the younger, slimmer, and quite a bit taller one, was Taas. He was one of their own. The stocky, powerful man was called The Stranger. Had they known his name, it would not have been customary for them to use it. The tribe spoke only among themselves. Life was safer that way.

Taas and The Stranger were working — and arguing — halfway up an almost sheer cliff, at the mouth of a very large cave. One of the more adventurous single males had discovered it two years ago, and the tribe had lived in it for several weeks. But they'd moved on because it was hard to get to. No fewer than three different ladders were needed on the north side and four on the south to get up from the bank of the river that flowed along the bottom. From the top of the cliff, the cave was completely inaccessible except with ropes.

Still, there were positive features, and had Saan, their leader, been successful in his attempts to build enthusiasm, the tribe would have stayed longer. The cave was dry. It faced east, and thus caught the sun in the morning, when it was most needed. There was no evidence of use by bears or cougars, and a huge, flat ledge jutted out in front of it, making an ideal communal area. Just the type of place where the Red People would choose to build.

The Stranger was one of the Red People. That may or may not have been their true name, but it was the one the tribe used for the people to the west, with whom they traded their woven mats and baskets and cloth for axes and wedges and pestles and the like, fashioned from flint. They were good at flinting, the Red People. They were good at building, too, at carving and shaping and piling pieces of the endless red sandstone, so that a cave on a cliffside, if it were big enough, could be turned into a dwelling with many rooms. Perhaps more important, such a dwelling could easily become a kind of fortress, protection against the dreaded raiders from the north.

The concept of a home as a defensive structure, however, was only a vague one in the minds of most of the tribe, for home to them meant a convenient cave or copse of trees in the cold season; when it was hot and dry, just about any place near water would do. It had been Saan who had convinced them of the value of the cliff site as a permanent home and as a means of protection — a place that could be defended. Saan was the one who led the trading delegation west each spring to the confluence of the two rivers, where other peoples gathered to barter and exchange. Before Saan, his father, Lo-Tov, had been the leader and before that only a few could remember, for the elders were all dead now. Killed, all of them — Saan, too — by the raiders from the north.

Taas had accompanied the trading delegation the previous spring. He was young, and it was his first time. Although he had not been allowed to enter the Red People's dwelling place, he had seen it from the outside, and despite his youth and limited experience the value of the protection idea had impressed him. So had the discussion between Saan and the elders of the Red

People. Not that Taas had understood all of it, but he did grasp the notion that they, the Red People, were the motivators in getting all of the southern tribes to defend themselves. And when Saan later pointed out to the rest of the tribe that if all the peoples in this part of the desert were too strong for the raiders from the north, the raiders would simply stop coming, Taas, along with all the others, had embraced the idea.

But before they could act, there was yet another raid, the one that had taken Saan and all the elders, and it left Taas as the only one in the tribe with more than just a vague idea of what the defense project was all about. That's why it was he who worked with The Stranger when he came, and why it was Taas, now, who was arguing with him up on the wide ledge that projected from the cave. The two had spent several days piling stones artfully across the front of the cave, so that a half-finished wall with space left for a single entrance now reached as high as Taas's chest. It was a strong wall, for The Stranger had taught Taas how to use stones that fit naturally and, when they didn't, how to use the flint axes to change their shape. He'd taught the women and children how to make mortar, which, twice a day, they brought up from the river in the reed baskets they were so good at weaving and pushed into the joints between the stones, although as yet they had no idea whatsoever why this was necessary.

From below, their work to prepare the next batch of mortar was suspended now as they watched the dispute. It made them very nervous. They were unused to dealing with other people, and had watched their visitor's every movement with wary suspicion. From what they could tell, watching the two gesticulate, the disagreement had to do with the entrance. The Stranger had taken a long, narrow piece of red sandstone, shaped it with his flint axes into a rectangular design and had laid it across the entrance. Then he'd begun further construction of the wall across and above it. Taas, who was almost at the point of stamping his feet by this time, would point at the stone emphatically, an expression of complete frustration on his face, and then wave the same hand back and forth over his head, palm down, and parallel to the ledge. He would then stoop awkwardly from the waist several times. In response, The Stranger, too, would touch the long stone and, just like Taas, would stoop awkwardly and raise his hand above his head palm down. But his gesture ended with a hard slap to the top of his head.

Their motions had been repeated often enough now to appear almost ritualistic, but as the mutual frustration mounted, the gestures were becoming progressively more animated. The situation was turning dangerous and needed resolution.

? *The Stranger and Taas obviously disagree about the height of the entranceway. It should not be difficult to understand what Taas is asking for, but what is The Stranger's reasoning for wanting to top it at its current height?*

FILE # 5

Setting Up the Hit

He didn't say hello. Just, "You're late. You were supposed to call half an hour ago."

She tried to explain. "I got held up at th—"

"You work for me." The cut off was abrupt and rude. "When I say you're to call, you call. Doesn't matter what's going down, becau—"

"We're supposed to meet him at 5:00." She could play this game, too. He didn't frighten her. She knew the hit wouldn't come off without her. "It's now ten to four. Are we going to discuss the set-up? Or maybe you want to make me go stand in a corner someplace until I learn to behave?"

A long pause. The sound of slow breathing into the receiver. Finally he said, "What's the name of the restaurant?"

"It's called The Lemon Tree. Corner of Chapel and Max."

"Chapel and Max!" He was really upset this time. "That's right by the Standard Life building! The sidewalk'll be jammed there at 5:00. All those clerks and secretaries!"

"That's what you wanted, isn't it?" She was annoyed now, too. "Look! You said the shooter will be on foot. Those secretaries and clerks you're so worried about have just put in a day's work and they're going to be tired and walking heads down. There's snow on the way so nobody will be strolling. What do you want already? You want a nice empty street, so the shooter can really stick out? Besides, you hired him. Is he a pro or what?"

Another tense pause. Then, "This Lemon Tree . . . Fancy, but not too fancy? And it's light menu, right?"

Deliberately, she waited just a little bit longer than necessary, and then spoke just a touch more slowly than needed. "It feeds the downtown office crowd. Mostly fast lunches. Upscale wraps, rabbit food, stuff like that. Closes at 7:00, so they don't even have a dinner menu. Nobody takes your coat and fusses. None of that 'Hi! I'm your waiter' blather."

"But it takes reservations, surely? We need a table at the door, or the shooter walks right on by."

This time she almost lost it. "Are you *nuts*! Reservations? You want me to hang a flag on myself or maybe carry a sign so we can make *sure* the restaurant will remember us?"

"I didn't get most of that! You're breaking up."

Yeah, sure, she thought, but bit her tongue. They hadn't liked each other from the beginning, but a job was a job and squabbling would get them nowhere.

"Doesn't matter," she said. "Traffic's bad here. Can you hear me now?"

"All clear now."

"We don't need a reservation. I'll be across the street from The Lemon Tree in about half an hour. There are two tables for four right by the door, so when one's free — that won't be a problem, guaranteed — I'll grab it. He'll be on time — apparently he's a punctuality freak — so you join me by five to five, right? So we can make sure he sits in the only seat with its back to the door?"

"As we planned," he replied. His voice was much calmer now, too, as though the need to cooperate had occurred to him at the same time. "And when I see the shooter," he continued, "I excuse myself and go to the restroom. You get up to find a waiter."

"Right. That covers it. See you, then, in . . ." She looked at the clock on the dashboard. ". . . in fifty-five minutes."

He didn't say good-bye either.

? *The woman in the conversation above provides a clue as to how she and the man she is speaking to will make sure the victim sits with his back to the door. How will it be done?*

FILE # 6

Under the
Home Team Bench

With a grimy index finger, Fritz Lang pulled back the tangle of leaves and vines to get a better look at the game but immediately drew back, violently slamming both his elbows into his stomach. He was all too familiar with the symptoms of malaria and knew that without quinine there was no way he'd stave off the delirium that was sure to come. Fritz pushed his arms into his body even harder to squeeze the chill rolling up through his torso. It worked this time, helped along by rapid breathing, but it wouldn't be long, he knew, before the strange visions would begin, and the dizziness. Then would come the sweats and the blackouts. He needed quinine.

It was out there, he knew, waiting for him just a short distance away. In a bag, a tattered little blue canvas sack. On the edges of Fritz's feverish brain, the last words of the senior agent were playing and replaying like a broken tape recorder.

"You've got a two-hour window at the airstrip seven days from now. If you're not there, we go, and you'll have to get out on the river. There'll be a cache set up for that, just in case. The canvas-bag routine; you know it. Pesos for bribes. Some bolivars, too, because you're pretty close to the Venezuelan border, but

I doubt you'll need them. Astronaut food. Quinine. The usual. Once you're on the river, it should be a pretty quick run to the coast for a jungle man like you."

That was two weeks ago. Fritz had found the cocaine processing lab they'd been looking for, so in that sense it was mission accomplished, but he'd been too late for the airplane and had had to go to the backup escape plan. Whether it was because of the extra time in the Colombian jungle, or whether his body was simply due no matter what, this morning Fritz Lang's malaria had returned full bore.

He leaned forward again into the vines, put out his finger tentatively, and waited. No chills this time. He leaned forward a little more. Still okay. He reached all the way and pulled the vines aside. Now he could really see and hear the crowd. Amazing, he thought, what a filter the jungle is. Only about fifty yards from the edge of the growth where he was hiding, the soccer game — uh, the *football* game; *get it right*, this is South America! — the football game had attracted the whole town. Yet he was barely aware anyone was there.

Or maybe it was the malaria. Through the buzz that was continually gathering strength in his brain, Fritz could hear the agent again. "Blue canvas bag, the same kind we always use, with a piece of duct tape on it. Our man will have it under the home team bench, if you can call it a bench. The facilities there are about as low end as they come. Soccer's huge in all these countries — you know they call it 'football'? — and every little village has a team and a cow pasture with goal posts."

Another sudden chill grabbed Fritz at the waist and rushed up to encircle his chest. He sat back, hugging himself again, forcing the shakes to stop by sheer will power. But he couldn't stop the buzzing; it was like a million tiny insects in his head, insects that were chewing at . . . No, not insects! The noise — it was the crowd! They were yelling about something. For the third time, he made a window for himself, wider this time. Somebody score a goal? No . . . well, maybe. A tall, extremely thin player was running along the sidelines with both hands in the air. Yes, he was the one the crowd was cheering. The player stopped under the goal posts and pumped a single fist into the air, raising the crowd to a frenzy. Twice, after he'd sat down with his team, he had to stand and salute the crowd before it turned to the game once more.

Now Fritz had a better understanding of something the agent had said.

"Wait till the end of the game," he'd instructed. "You got maybe ten, fifteen seconds if you play it right. Doesn't matter who wins or loses, the place'll go nuts and everybody'll go out on the field. Could be you'll even get lucky and there'll be a brawl. Anyway, chances are about zero that you'll be noticed if you act like they do. So you get in, get the bag, and get out. From the field you're not more than five minutes to the river, so . . . Now, if worse comes to worst, forget about the bag altogether. You can still make it without the pesos."

But not without the quinine. Fritz studied the field, trying to take in as much as he could before the next chill grabbed him. Directly in front of him, fifty yards away, were the goal posts where the player had danced a few seconds ago. The crowd was big for a simple village game; Fritz estimated several hundred at least. And it was a shabby place. At the other end of the field, a small red splash on top of a stake suggested that Coca Cola had once sponsored a scoreboard, but that was long gone now. There was a well-worn players' bench on either side of the field at what would have been the center line had there been one, but there were no bleachers for the fans, not even seats. A few tattered canvas chairs were scattered about, but they stood empty, for the majority of the crowd milled along the sidelines, constantly on the move with the play, competing for the best view. The players didn't even have uniforms. Both teams wore a ragtag mix of different colors. Obviously, you had to be local to know which team was which. The paramilitaries were well equipped though. With camouflage suits and the ever-present AK-47s, they patrolled in pairs.

One thing the agent may have underestimated, Fritz thought. Unless he actually ran directly in and out, thereby attracting attention, it would take more than ten or fifteen seconds to grab the sack and get back to the jungle. All in all, this was not a good deal. If it weren't for the quinine . . . Fritz withdrew his hand and allowed the vines to settle over him again. He had to get as much of an advantage as he could, so his next move would be to slip around through the jungle to the home team side. When the game ended, he would have to be as close to their bench as possible. Now, he mouthed silently to himself, which side has the home team bench?

 Since there are only two benches, one on either side of the field, Fritz Lang has a fifty-fifty chance of picking the home team one correctly, but logic should improve the odds considerably. How can he tell which bench is most likely to be the home team's?

FILE # 7

First Impressions Revised

Of the four people at the round conference table, it was not hard to tell that the one in charge was the woman with straight, gray hair, the one with the sharply tailored uniform and the double loop of gold cord on her shoulder. She was a large woman, but the ease with which she carried her body reinforced her obvious comfort with command. Across from her, two of the others, no milquetoasts themselves, showed their respect in the level of care in their speech. They addressed the large woman only as "Chief Voltz," for example. Not "Chief" or "Ma'am," but "Chief Voltz," as if a natural bond connected her title and her name. The two were Detective First Grade Levitt Furst and Chief Medical Examiner Marjorie Schenk. They were in civilian clothes.

The fourth person, like the chief, was in uniform. He was a balding man with glasses who somehow managed to look like he was sitting beside and behind his boss at the same time. The man was as slight as the chief was large and, in an earlier time, would never have made the height requirements for a police force. His title was Office Assistant to the Chief, and his name was Mervyn Rivers, although he was widely known at headquarters as "Miss Brooks."

The meeting had been going on for thirty minutes already and Rivers had yet to say anything. It looked, too, as if any opportunity to contribute would soon end, for Chief Voltz had just made an expansive terminating gesture with her arm to look at her watch.

"Press conference in five minutes." She held Furst and Schenk alternately with her gaze. "It could be one of the most important we've held in the past several years. Unless I can offer a reason for them to think otherwise, the press is going to have a police scandal to drool over. I don't have to tell you the headlines: 'Precinct Captain Handcuffs and Strangles Wife. Then Shoots Self!' Of course," she added, bitterly, "the fact that he is — was — the first black captain in the history of the force is icing on the cake. As if that's not enough, the wife's white, and — *and* — she was having an affair! A mess!"

She drew a long, audible breath, then exhaled even more noisily. "Once more," she said. "Tell me one more time."

Detective Furst opened his notebook, although he knew the details by heart. It helped him detach his eyes from those of his boss. He began. "The driver waits by the sidewalk at 7:15 this morning, like every other morning. When Max doesn't show up, he goes to the door. It's open. Max and Beatty had a small den just off the front foyer. Place for reading, watching TV, and that. He looks in there and they're both dead. Or look dead, anyway. He calls . . . er . . . how much detail do you want, Chief Voltz? Do you want me to . . ."

"Keep going." Chief Voltz swept her watch arm round again. "I'll interrupt if I have to."

"Yes." Furst cleared his throat. "I arrived on the scene at 7:48 with . . ."

"Never mind who else. What did you see? First impression."

Furst cleared his throat again. "First impression is murder/suicide. Beatty is on the floor, her back to the door. Of course, the first thing I see is the cuffs. She's cuffed behind her back." The detective looked at the chief uneasily. "They're Max's cuffs, Chief Voltz. Or at least . . . well, they're our issue, and his prints are on them."

The chief's expression did not change. "Keep going," she said again.

"There are heavy welts and marks around her neck. We found a kid's skipping rope underneath her. What . . . what it looks like . . . is he cuffed her and then . . . it looks like he choked her."

"And Max?" Underneath the gold braid, the chief rotated her shoulder slightly, a habit of hers when she was becoming impatient. "Ate his gun then, right?"

Detective Furst was not finding this easy. "It appears he put the barrel in his mouth and . . . he was lying a few feet away. We estimate it all happened between about 10:00 last night and midnight." He looked at Marjorie Schenk for confirmation.

"That's right, Chief Voltz," the medical examiner picked up the narrative. "The thermostat was set unusually high in the house and the heat made it hard to be more precise than that."

Schenk paused until Voltz nodded to go on.

"Everything I found is consistent with the interpretation of events as Detective Furst describes them." Marjorie Schenk tended to lapse into a witness-box style at moments like these.

"The entry and exit wounds on Captain Winters . . . er . . . Max . . . are consistent with self-inflicted harm. Entry in roof of the mouth. Exit at the top of the skull with significant damage. The top and back of the skull are pretty much destroyed."

"He used a dum-dum?" the chief wanted to know.

"We found it in the wall, Chief Voltz." Detective Furst interjected. "Too smashed up to be sure, but it looks like it."

Voltz sighed. "What next? Now we've got a upper-level member of the force with illegal bullets." She sighed again. "Go on, Marjorie."

"Except for the cause of death factors, there are no other wounds or marks at all on Cap— Max. The same is true for the wife. The ligature marks on the neck, however, are significant. Intense pressure applied just below the larynx."

"Then he didn't kill her." The room went starkly silent. It was "Miss Brooks." The others looked at him and then at each other as if they had heard an echo.

"Miss Brooks" carried on, eyes fixed firmly on the surface of the table. "It's evident Captain Winters did not strangle Mrs. Winters. In fact, what is more likely is that a third person killed them both, and has made it appear to be a murder/suicide. Perhaps to embarrass the force. That's only my opinion, of course."

 On what basis does "Miss Brooks" conclude — correctly — that Captain Max Winters did not strangle his wife?

FILE # 8

Collecting a Betrayal Fee

Yesterday afternoon, one of the big double doors to her father's study had been slightly ajar, and Sophie Andros had slipped in and taken half a million dollars in bearer bonds from the wall safe.

Call it a betrayal fee, Daddy. For what you did to me and Mom. I just wish she were still around to enjoy this.

Sophie wasn't sure she believed in God any more, but she had to admit that the door being open yesterday suggested a force of some kind trying to tip things in her favor. Oh, she'd planned to do *something* if she ever got back into this house. Just what she didn't know, but yesterday everything happened so naturally and so easily, and she hadn't even had a plan!

To begin with, she'd shown up at the house for the first time in twenty-four years, and nobody had answered the front door.

OK, so I wasn't expected until today. But see, I knew Aspen would be out. You could be taking your last breath, Daddy, but she wouldn't miss her spa day, would she? And what the heck! Twenty-four years! I wanted to prowl around a bit.

She'd stood in the cavernous foyer for the longest time, taking in all the remembered sounds and smells.

Not the sights, though, Daddy. Not a thing here I remember. "Decorator Queen," Mom used to call her. I can see why.

When there was still no response, she had walked around the wide sweeping staircase and down a dark hallway to where a huge pair of oak doors with brass knobs in the shape of lions' heads marked the entrance to Constantine Andros's study. The door on the right was open, and she'd gone in.

And there you were, Daddy. In the same chair you were sitting in when Mom took me away that day. I was crying so hard. Mostly because I didn't understand. All I knew was Aspen was in and Mom was out. Like trading in a car for a newer, shinier model. Do you even remember, Daddy? You didn't know me yesterday, but then you don't know anybody any more, do you?

Constantine Andros had been sitting at his desk yesterday, his back to a fireplace scoured of its carbon and ashes. Like the rest of the study, it had a look, not of neglect, but of disuse. Like a no-touch diorama in a museum, where the curators had succeeded in capturing and holding a moment in time. Constantine was part of the display. No movement. An empty stare. Only the shallowest of breaths. He'd been placed in the chair by a curator of his own, a nurse who, as though to confirm Sophie's sense of a mysterious, balancing force, was suffering from stomach cramps and had left the old man to go to the bathroom.

How I used to love that room! You let me go in there — the only one allowed to, because I was your favorite. You were my favorite too, Daddy. And it was such a room! All the books . . . books from floor to ceiling, that big, ugly moose head over the mantel, and great big chairs. And the smells — leather and sherry, the fireplace. The bay window . . . my spot! I'd lie there on the window seat with the morning sun in my face and watch the birds feeding in the gazebo. You knew the name of every bird, too, didn't you? Do you know any of them now?

Sophie had walked slowly around the study, touching this, feeling that. She went over to the bay window and looked out, shaking her head slightly. The yard . . . it had seemed so huge when she was little. Had it shrunk? Did backyards get smaller in twenty-four years? Her father had certainly shrunk. The strokes had seen to that.

You didn't even move when I opened the safe, Daddy! Remember how you taught me? It was our secret! Left 27, right 14, left 45, right 6, right 20. I remembered it all these years. And you know, as soon as I saw the room, as soon as I saw it was the one spot in the house that Aspen didn't touch, I knew the combination wouldn't have changed either. So . . .

She had left as undetected and unnoticed as she'd arrived and now Sophie was here again. This time for her expected, official visit. The nurse answered the door before she'd even put her finger to the chimes. Now Sophie stood in front of Constantine Andros's study again. This time the double doors were closed. Sophie thought she heard voices inside, but couldn't be sure, although she knew Aspen was in there, and Kimberley, the half-sister she'd seen only once, and the lawyer. Him she knew.

"Stavros the Mortician," Mom always called him. He's been around forever. Before Aspen, even before Mom. He's the one I have to watch out for. If anybody knows the bonds are gone, it's him. And if anybody is going to suspect me . . . him again. Just be cool, Sophie. Remember, you haven't been in this room in twenty-four years. Don't give them any reason to think otherwise.

With one knuckle extended, Sophie tapped very timidly on the door.

"Come in! We're waiting!" Stavros's gravelly voice came through the doors.

Sophie tugged hard several times at the lion's head on the right door.

"The other door!"

Good start! It's obvious I don't know which of the doors is used.

Greetings followed under a thin veil of politeness.

Aspen spoke. "It's a wee bit late for it, but I was just about to make our afternoon tea, Sophia. May I include you?"

"Please."

For heaven's sake, don't mumble! Be confident!

"Recognize anything, little Sophie?" Stavros asked.

Sophie bit her tongue. He was trying to be polite.

OK. Now be a bit overwhelmed. The memories are flooding back!

"The old moose . . . is it still . . . ?" She turned almost a full circle. "Why, there it . . . Was it always over the mantel? I thought it used to be . . . no . . . I'm not sure. This is so . . . so strange."

Keep looking around. Slowly, slowly. Stare a bit. Whatever you do, don't stare at the A.Y. Jackson painting. The one that hides the wall safe.

"Ah, little Sophie, everything in here has been the same for thirty years or more. It's got your father's stamp."

"Er . . . where is my . . . he?"

"Nurse is taking him out to the gazebo," Kimberley explained.

"Nurse"! "Nurse" for heaven's sake! As if this were a Victorian manor!

"We aren't sure, but we think he still rather enjoys the birds." The half-sister continued with more speculation on Constantine's likes and dislikes, but Sophie wasn't listening. As though she couldn't resist the temptation, she went over to the bay window, perched sideways on the edge of the window seat and looked out to the gazebo, shading her eyes against the lowering sun to see better.

Yes, but does Nurse ("Nurse" . . . gawd!) identify the birds for him. That's what would make him really happy.

". . . Before the most recent stroke a couple of years ago," Kimberley was still talking as Sophie came back to the chair that had been set out for her, "he had the gazebo moved to the other side of the yard to get away from the traffic noises. There's a lot of traffic now that the city opened the . . ."

Why she's as nervous as I am, prattling on like that. This is going to be easier than I thought, so just stay cool.

It was not until she saw Stavros staring at her that Sophie realized her mistake.

 What did Sophie do that made Stavros realize she has been here more recently than twenty-four years ago?

Nobody Hides Forever

From the south, a nondescript brown sedan came into view on the two-lane highway and then eased off onto a lightly travelled secondary road forking to the east. Soon the car entered an area of thick forest and turned right again onto a narrow laneway leading up to a squat gray building made of cement block. The building was even more nondescript than the sedan, its monotony only slightly relieved by a metal garage door and, above it on a second floor, a window of thick plate glass.

Behind the window, Norm Upshur lowered the binoculars he had been using to follow the progress of the car. He watched intently as a very large man in mechanic's coveralls got out of the back seat of the sedan on the passenger side. A frail man with tousled white hair got out right after him, followed by another large man in coveralls. The small man wore brown plaid trousers with a brown check. He had on a plaid shirt under a thin, two-tone windbreaker, and cheap running shoes. Old man's clothes. At the sound of the garage door opening, the three men disappeared into the building, and the car went back down the dirt road into the forest.

Norm set the binoculars on the window ledge. "So that's Lazlo

Bovic?" He stared out at the trees for a few thoughtful seconds before turning behind him to a man sitting on an upturned crate in front of a makeshift desk. "Hard to believe that little old man is the Butcher of Vojvodina. In fact, Harland, now that I've seen him, I have to tell you I'm even more unconvinced."

Harland Stohl had the kind of face on which a smile would look out of place. True to form, he scowled and said, "That's Bovic. And he's been living in this country since 1947. According to our data . . ."

"Your data, Harland, with all due respect, have gotten us into trouble more than once."

"Then take a look for yourself." Stohl was unperturbed. "Start with this photograph. We have others, taken since he came here in '47, but this one is earlier. From his days in Croatia during the war. The only one we know of. We got it from an old woman in Bosnia."

"See, Harland, there we are to start with. That old woman who gave you the picture . . . she's actually a Bosnian *Serb*, isn't she? That makes her no friend of the Croats, I'll grant you, but then she's no friend of ours, either! What does she have to gain by exposing him? The Serbs committed war crimes of their own!"

Stohl carried on with no sign of impatience. "The Balkans," he said, and shrugged as if that explained everything. When Upshur didn't respond, he added, "Serbs and Croats have been fighting each other for a thousand years, but every once in a while they let bygones be bygones and get together to gang up on Bosnia. Maybe her motive is some political one we don't understand yet."

He shrugged again. "Or maybe it's religious. The woman is a Catholic like Bovic, but she's Orthodox; most Serbs are, those that aren't Muslim. Bovic, like most of the Croats, is Roman Catholic." He sighed very softly, as though he'd had to slog through this explanation many times before. "Usually, in the Balkans that's all the reason you need, but in this case I think she's turned him in because she's a dyed-in-the-wool communist, an old *partisan*.

Probably has something to do with the war. World War II, I mean. They're about the same age, her and Bovic."

Norm bent over slightly, trying to look into the other man's eyes as if they held the key to sorting out his uncertainty. "And old Bovic downstairs," he said, "if he really is Bovic, was a leader of the *ustashi*, poster boys for the Gestapo and the SS. For the *ustashi*, slaughtering communists — *partisans* — was almost a religion."

Harland shrugged a third time. "People on this side of the Atlantic have no idea how bad it was. They know over there, though. And they never forget."

He turned the photograph around so that Norm Upshur could see it right side up. "Here. Just take a look. Our people say it was taken about 1943."

Norm Upshur glanced at the tattered photograph for only a second. "He's shaving, Harland, for heaven sake!"

For once Harland Stohl showed a bit of spirit. "You were expecting a cigarette ad, maybe? Why not shaving? Or eating? Or drinking? Or sitting on the toilet! Think of it. Bovic's a key player in the *ustashi* in a country where there are any number of factions all trying to kill one another, where nobody trusts anybody — they still don't! — so this had to be with a hidden camera. What better time than when he's shaving?"

"Makes sense, I suppose." Norm agreed with more than a little reluctance. "This the scar?"

"Precisely in the middle of the forehead. And precisely where there's one on the old boy downstairs, as you'll soon see."

"The medal on that chain around his neck . . . Says I-H . . . Can't make out the . . ."

Stohl handed Upshur a magnifying glass. "An 'S.' Catholics all over the world wear that. Stands for *in hoc signo*. Means 'in this sign.' Refers to the cross where Jesus was crucified."

Norm handed back the glass and returned to the window, where only a few minutes earlier he had watched the approach of the car. He was still very troubled. "I don't know, Harland. A forty-year-old photograph and an old commie woman with a grudge . . . and, wait a minute! Let me see that thing again! Yes! He's shaving with his right hand!" Norm came around to Harland's side of the desk. He tapped the photograph with an insistent index finger. "What that means . . . what it means is — in a mirror — what it means is he's left-handed! Now the old guy downstairs . . . is he right- or left-handed, because . . . ?"

"I know what you're getting at." Harland Stohl shook his head. "One of the first things we looked at, but it doesn't apply here. You saw that yourself."

 Why does Norm Upshur assume that Bovic is left-handed, and why, as Harland Stohl says, does it not apply here?

The Initiation

Thirty-two years I been at this. Went into narcotics right out of the academy. Undercover. Traffic after that — talk about a switch! Then I did bunko, vice for three years, and before I turned private I was in homicide. Made sergeant. Don't get me wrong, this isn't bragging. I just want you to know I been around the block. Seen it all. Every con artist, beater, dipper, shooter, weirdo, and just plain dumb crook there is. That's what I thought, anyway. Until Mrs. Kumar-White.

Oh, she wasn't weird or anything. Better get that straight right away. In fact, she was pretty classy. A looker and a real sharp dresser. Not flashy either. Tasteful. Made you look twice. Sure turned heads in the building where I got my office. We don't get her type down there. I got to tell you that made me suspicious at first. You see, I do a lot of husband chasing. It's bread and butter in my business. And women like her — they usually phone. Look you up in the yellow pages or get a referral from one of their friends. But her, she just shows up at my office. No appointment, nothing.

'Course I bring her in right away or she'd have drawn a crowd out in the hall. And she sits down and starts right in.

"My husband," she says.

Now, it turns out to be one of your standard I-think-my-husband-is-playing-around cases, but most women, they dance around the subject first. Like they don't actually want to *say* it? Or else they want to know about my fee. Stuff like that. Not her.

"My husband," she starts. "I think my husband is being kidnapped."

You can see already, can't you, this is weird? *"Being* kidnapped"? Oh yeah. I should tell you right up front here that the whole thing was good old-fashioned infidelity. The guy — White — he was having not one but *two* adventures on the side. But the weird part is how this all played out.

'Course I tell her she should be seeing the police if it's a snatch, though I can just hear the guys cracking up as soon as she tells them *"being* kidnapped." But then she explains. Says it's like a cult thing.

"He's always been a joiner," she says. "It's like he was disappointed when he got too old for Boy Scouts. He's a Shriner. He belongs to the Rotary Club. He's a Mason. He especially likes the secret ones with the special handshakes and the ceremonies and the funny clothes."

So far I'm not hearing a thing that interests me and if it weren't that she was the best looking client I've had in that office for longer than I can remember, I'd have been looking for an escape hatch. But then what she does is, she reaches into her purse and brings out a wad of hundreds. Counts out ten of them.

"Will one thousand be a sufficient advance?" she asks.

I don't tell her that most of the time I have to squeeze to get a couple of hundred out of a client so she's got my attention.

OK, so now I'm interested, and then she says, "I want you to become a member of the Simon Pure Society, like my husband. And tell me how I can get him back, before they take him from me completely."

Now here's where it goes right off the track. Seems this Simon Pure Society — oh, there really is one; that's the first thing I look into — it's full of these nutbars playing head games all the time.

You see, every member is either a total liar, never ever tells the truth — Simon Pure, get it? — or else they swing the other way, tell the truth every single time no matter what. Different kind of pure, see? And to be a member you got to be one or the other; can't be both! Look, don't quit on me here, I'm not making this up!

Anyway, to make a long story short, I go visit this Simon Pure Society. They got a spot down by the lake, just off Carrick. Mrs. Kumar-White gets me a referral — I'm still working out how that happened — 'cause you can't just walk in off the street. I make them think I'm interested in joining and I pay a fee so I can take the initiation. Three hundred bucks, so maybe not all of them are nuts!

It's set up for the next afternoon and I show up early. A habit of mine, good one, too, 'cause I got to see White, the husband, with these two chippies all over him. Got a coupla pictures so that was the end of that. Last I heard he had joined the Eternal Alimony Society. The Mrs. saw to that. But let me finish on this Simon Pure thing. By now I'm really into this weird deal. Want to see if it's for real.

So they take me into a sort of lounge. This was no saloon by the way. Very posh. I'm taken to a table for four and then in come these three, a guy and two women. They sit down at my table, don't say a word to me, and a waiter comes, takes orders for drinks. I order soda water. Got to be clear for this.

Now I should explain — and stay with me, I thought this was nuts, too, when I first heard it: Like I told you, if you join Simon Pure, you got to go one way or the other full time, so you choose to be either a Fabrican or a Veritan depending on whether you want to lie all the time or tell the truth. Fabricans are the liars and . . . well, you can figure it out. Everybody's dead serious, by the way. They got this system of increasing fines, for example, if you're caught out of character. You only get three strikes before you're tossed out for a while. All part of the game. You see, everybody knows what everybody else is, so the big thing is to catch someone saying something the wrong way.

Anyway, what I have to do in the initiation is figure out which one of my three testers is the Veritan, because there will be only one at the table. Each of them will speak once and only once. And then I get one shot only; my first answer is my final answer. So we sit there for the longest time. They don't say anything and I'm getting a little nervous. There's this really awful music playing. Loud, too, very distracting.

After a while I can't take it any more so I ask, "Which one of you is the Veritan?"

Again there's this long silence, then suddenly one of the women speaks. No warning, no smile — no frown either — no body language. Doesn't even look at me, and says, "I'm the Veritan."

The others don't react. There's a pause again, and now the drinks come. Just as the waiter starts to set them down, the guy — he's across from me — says his bit. But I don't hear him 'cause the waiter drops the tray! All I hear is "I'm the . . ." So now I figure I'm in a fix, but then the other woman turns to me. She's actually quite friendly. Smiles a bit, not like the other two. Touches my arm just a little, like she's sorry about what happened with the tray.

And she says, "I'm the Veritan. Perry just told you that he is, but you shouldn't believe him." And she points to the first one. "Her either," she says.

And then just like that, they all get up and leave. Did I tell you this was weird or what?

By the way, even though I scored in the initiation — it really wasn't all that hard to pick the one Veritan — I never did join the Society. It's a nice place and all. That lounge was something. But the annual fee is fifteen hundred bucks! In my business I get to hear liars every day. For nothing!

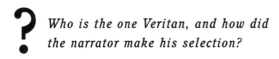

Who is the one Veritan, and how did the narrator make his selection?

Taking Over the
Thomas Case

The words of the chief prosecutor were scarcely five minutes old when Kirsten Oullette heard the promised tap on her door.

"I'll send up one of the paralegals with the Thomas case," he'd said. "This kid Loy has been helping Harry on it."

That was after a lame apology for dumping her into the stream so quickly. "I know you're brand new," he'd put it, "but with Harry's coronary you're the only assistant DA with space for his cases. You should be able to get up to speed without too much problem. Only Thomas that's urgent. Harry's had two continuances already on that one. If we ask for another, it'll get tossed for sure, so . . . We'll get you help if we can, but for now we're just going to have to make do."

A second, more insistent knock brought Kirsten back to the present and she called to her visitor to come in.

"Peter Loy from downstairs, Ms. Oullette." He pronounced it oo-lit, leaning hard on the first syllable. Normally Kirsten made people rehearse the French pronunciation until they got it right, but she decided this wasn't the time.

"CP said to bring you the Thomas material?" He stood hesitantly just inside the door. "And go over it with you? If you want?"

Kirsten's first thought was "he's even greener than I am," but she was still stinging from the chief prosecutor's unconscious insult about making do and was determined to work with what she was given without asking for help.

"Sit down," she said. "Yes, go over everything. From the beginning."

Grateful to be given some purpose, Peter Loy quickly settled himself and then pulled a large brown envelope from the stack he'd been carrying. It was full of photographs. "These are CS shots of the vic," he said. "Thought that would be a good place to start."

"C . . . S . . .?" Kirsten wrinkled her nose.

"Crime scene."

"Oh."

If Loy sensed her unfamiliarity, he didn't show it. "Now, here's the vic as he was found," he said as he put a photograph on the table. "Name's Velasquez, Martin Velasquez. Forty-two-year-old white male. Married, no children. Currency trader."

Kirsten was determined not to reveal further inexperience by reacting to the picture of a man who had been both bludgeoned and stabbed, but it took all her strength. What she forced herself to observe calmly was the body of a man in jogging shorts and top, lying in more blood than she had ever seen at one time.

"The CSA figures he was hit from behind first. On the back of the head."

"CSA?"

"Crime scene analyst. Anyway, seems the vic always stopped at this same spot for a breather, and the perp was waiting with a brick. We got it, the brick. I'll show you in a minute. Anyway, the vic goes down. Motive is robbery. Can you figure a guy like this? Jogging with cash? Not too bright, if you ask me, for a money guy. See, he always stopped for juice, Velasquez did, at this twenty-four-hour diner and always had a wad of cash. Anyway, the vic goes down, like I said, face first and then the perp rolls him over. That's why you can't see any wound on the head, but there's all that blood coming out the back."

Kirsten stared at the picture. She was afraid to blink.

"Now the CSA figures the vic comes to, or maybe he's not even out altogether so the perp stabs him. See all that blood that's come out of the chest?"

It didn't make her feel good, but Kirsten could see all too well.

"The ME says the stab is the cause of death. That's why the public defender is making noises about a plea bargain down to manslaughter. Lack of intent. Anyway, here's blood on the shorts. The CSA says that's the perp wiping his knife. And those marks on the arm? The scratches? No blood on those, d'ya notice? Anyway, that's the perp ripping off a Rolex. We didn't find the knife, by the way, but the Rolex is downstairs in the evidence stores."

Kirsten didn't miss the "we."

"ME puts TOD at between 4:00 and 5:00 a.m. That's another thing! Can you imagine somebody jogging out there that early? Wife says he was a jogging freak, besides being a workaholic."

Loy turned his attention to the materials still on his lap. "Now for the perp," he said. "There was fog down by the lake that morning and the body's off the path. Wasn't found till almost 9:00, so you'd expect the perp'd be long gone, but not this guy."

He pulled a face-on/profile mug shot from another envelope. "Here's our man, nature's contribution to the left side of the bell curve. Eliot Dickinson Thomas."

"Any chance he speaks in rhyming couplets?" Kirsten ventured.

The blank stare said Loy didn't get the little joke and she didn't bother to explain.

"What's his story?" she asked instead.

"Your typical NFA."

At least she was familiar with "no fixed address."

"Homicide puts out the word down by the lake and over by the tracks, and, doesn't take long, this skell comes up with a tip there's a guy with a Rolex at the Savior Shelter, and it's Thomas. He's got a sheet a mile long, but this is the first major. Thomas admits taking the watch that morning, but he says the vic was already dead."

Kirsten tapped the mug shot with her pen. "Who else besides you and Harry have gone over this file?" she asked. "I mean, really carefully."

"Just us," Loy replied. "Well really, mostly me because Harry, he was sick for a long time before he had that, like, heart attack. Why?"

"Because there's evidence here that Thomas is telling the truth."

? *What evidence suggests that*
Thomas is telling the truth?

A Career Adjustment for Lonnie the "Dipper"

When Lonnie Baggins was working, which was usually at crowded airports or bus terminals — parades and championship games were also favored sites — he generally altered his appearance in one of several ways. They weren't exactly disguises, these alterations. Lonnie preferred to call them "enhancements." It was a word he had learned years ago and he liked it. He was careful not to use the same enhancement more than once at the same working site. And, after several uses, each would be abandoned in favor of a new one, even if the old one was particularly good. Lonnie was disciplined about that.

He had hated giving up the wig, for example. Although it was truly ugly, and looked more like worn-out Astroturf than hair, it had been very effective. So were the earrings some years ago, but he'd given them up even before they had become an everyday fashion. However, he continued to use false teeth and a moustache, sometimes singly, sometimes in combination. Lonnie's eyes were close set and his thin nose was so short that early in life he'd acquired "Rat" as a nickname. (His educated friends — there were two — called him "Ferret.") Still, with the teeth and moustache, Lonnie had turned an otherwise unfortunate feature into an advantage: On him, they were true enhancements of an appearance already established by nature.

Indeed it was his face that, among professional pickpockets, had made him somewhat of a contrarian. (Had he known that word, he'd have used it liberally. Lonnie's passion for words was fervent.) Most "dippers" try to blend in; the very last thing they want is to attract attention. But Lonnie didn't have much choice. He was already noticeable. And at least the alterations meant no one noticed his delicate, long-fingered hands, nature's compensating gift, the one that had made him one of the best at what he did.

Still, as a career support, the practice of altering the way he looked had not been a complete success. Lonnie had done two stretches in one of Her Majesty's institutions, although at heart he felt one of them didn't really count. It was at a "borstal" when he was seventeen, and, for people from the neighborhood where he grew up, a little time in juvenile detention was part of growing up.

On the other hand, neither experience had been very enjoyable. The two years at Tanningshire had turned out to be particularly unpleasant. Therefore, when the security bloke from British Airways approached him with a proposal — a legal, above-board proposal — about consulting for the company on passenger protection, he'd jumped at the chance before even considering the possible traps.

"What we want," the security man had said in his offer, "is your . . . er . . . professional — well, rather, the *benefit* of your *experience*. You see, the number of passengers losing their wallets and purses has increased dramatically of late. And . . . er . . . what we would like is . . . er . . . well, we would like to retain you for purposes of security analysis. Quietly, however. You see, British Airways is taking a lead here. We are not experiencing any more theft than any other airline, but the problem is worsening, so it's our wish to take some remedial steps without in any way attracting negative publicity either to the company or to air travel in general."

Lonnie liked "remedial steps" and mentally filed it away where he kept "enhancements."

"To begin," the British Airways man explained at their first official consultation a week later, "perhaps you could comment on the potential utility of the measures we're planning to initiate prior to the next peak travel period."

After "potential utility" Lonnie knew he should have followed his instincts and brought a notebook. "Initiate" he was already familiar with, but just to hear it used so comfortably gave him a pleasant buzz.

"In the first place, there will be an insert in every airline ticket issued. It's a short paragraph warning the traveler about pickpockets and offering some advice."

He handed a sheet of paper to Lonnie.

"I'll want you to review it. That's a rough draft of the paragraph you have there. Well, more than rough. As far as we're concerned, that's the penultimate state, pending your review."

Lonnie felt a warm glow at "penultimate."

"Secondly," the security man continued, "we will be posting this warning sign at key points in airports."

He handed another sheet to Lonnie.

"It's a briefer version of the insert and will be put up at luggage carousels, check-in counters, by the car-hire. Places like that. Thirdly, we will be increasing the number of uniformed personnel in those same key areas. Greater visibility, of course. An obvious preventative measure."

Lonnie merely nodded, but inside he felt a sense of satisfaction. He'd been expecting "preventative measure."

"And there's a fourth undertaking. I am especially interested in your opinion of this one. It has been proposed that we add non-uniformed personnel — undercover, sort of — specifically to watch for pickpocketing. Frankly, I have grave doubts as to whether the measure is truly an enhancement."

Lonnie's close-set eyes moistened ever so slightly, and the tiny nostrils flared.

The British Airways man was still talking. "You see, it's my

position that placing both uniformed and non-uniformed personnel in the same area is counter-productive. At the very least,
one of them will be redundant."

For Lonnie, this meeting had turned into a verbal diamond
mine. There were so many gems floating about in his head that
right then and there he almost blurted out the serious mistake
the security people were making. He'd tell them eventually, of
course, but not at the moment. No career criminal, dipper or any
other kind, could resist the opportunity to extend a potential
cash flow. And with all the delicious new words and phrases . . . !
Lonnie was straining to contain himself.

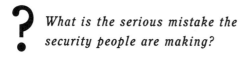

*What is the serious mistake the
security people are making?*

FILE # 13

A Second Witness

Neither police officer said a thing until the sound of wheel-chair tires had faded down the hallway toward the front of the house. Then they both began to speak at once, but Sal Forto, as usual, won out. He was the junior of the pair but far more assertive.

"Have you ever *seen* this many CDs!" he said. "I mean, outside of a store? There's gotta be five hundred or more!"

"Five hundred on that wall alone." Joy Weng was more careful, more analytical in her style. "There's at least that many on the next wall. And look at those shelves under the windows there, the ones facing the street. Another five hundred or so. I'd say more like a couple of thousand in total. Bet they're all classical too, like that radio station he's got on. This is a guy whose life is music."

Her comments didn't make a dent in Sal's focus.

"And the equipment!" Sal went down on one knee in front of an elaborate but very compact receiver and adjusted the tuning knob. The LED display moved a single decimal point and suddenly the fuzziness overlaying the sounds of a Mozart piano concerto disappeared like magic. "Classé," he said, then noticing her frown, added, "the receiver. It's top of the line. I'll bet those are Apogee speakers. The ones set into the wall there."

Joy Weng nodded. She was never able to rouse enthusiasm about things the way her partner could, but she was accustomed to his ramblings.

"I'll do the questioning, you hear? When he comes back?" she said. "He's got a perfect view through those windows. Not even a tree or a shrub between here and the hit-and-run site."

"Look at this! These are all jazz! Charley Parker, Stan Getz, Gershwin, Diana Krall, Gershwin again, Django Reinhart . . ." Sal was down on both knees now, examining one of the shelves of carefully stacked compact discs.

"'Course, he could have been reading the newspaper. There's today's *Post* on the ottoman." Joy continued her analysis.

"Miles Davis. Must be . . . four, five, *eight* Miles Davis! No, here's some more! Wonder why he doesn't have them in alphabetical order?"

"But then, even if he was reading the paper, surely the sound would have attracted his attention when the driver hit the brakes."

"Ah! Here's the Mozart and the classical stuff!" Sal Forto had turned the corner, still on his knees, and was now reading CD labels along the next wall.

"Sal, don't you think the guy's been in the bathroom an awfully long time?"

"Here it's Bach, Beethoven, Berlioz, Brahms, Bruch . . . Funny, he's got the classical ones in alphabetical order."

"*Sal!*"

"What?"

"Get on your feet! He's coming back!"

The sound of wheelchair tires on a hardwood floor announced the return of Dwayne Bolger. His house was the third call for Joy Weng and Sal Forto on the west side of Mount Pleasant Road. They had been assigned to canvass the houses on this side of the street for possible witnesses to a hit and run that had taken place a very short time before, critically injuring a little boy. The 9-1-1 call had come from the sole occupant of the next house but one to the south, on the same side as Bolger. According to this witness, a very elderly and quite feeble old lady, the car that hit the boy was white but she was not able to offer much more.

"One of those foreign-looking things," she'd said. And then she'd added — quite reasonably, Joy thought — "although they all look foreign these days now, don't they?"

No one answered the doorbell at the house between the old lady and Bolger, and the two officers had almost given up at his house, too, when his voice came through a speaker beside the door, directing them to open up and come in. He'd met them in the foyer in his wheelchair.

"I know why you're here," he'd said. "I've been expecting you. It's the accident, isn't it?" Upon which he motioned them into the room where they now stood, and announced he was on the way to the bathroom and would be right back.

"I saw the whole thing," Dwayne Bolger said as he wheeled into the room. "I've been in here all morning. Even saw you coming down the street. The child — it's the Anthony boy, isn't it? — he's always playing on the street. The car wasn't coming too fast, actually, not like some of them do on this street, but the child just darted out in front. A German car. Silver. A silver Jetta. Not that I know much about cars, but my son has a white Jetta. I would have called 9-1-1, but whoever used my telephone last didn't put it back." He pointed to an empty cradle for a cordless telephone. "Probably the cleaning lady. Does it all the time."

Out of the corner of her eye, Joy could see Sal looking at her intently. She knew he was itching to fire questions but she had said she would take the lead. It didn't really matter, however. Joy knew that Sal had caught the flaw in Bolger's account at the same time she did. They'd have to dig a bit to find out why he was lying, but the main work was done now.

What is the clue that makes Joy Weng and Sal Forto think Dwayne Bolger is not telling them the truth?

A Preview of
the Contract

Ordinarily, a closet would have been Charlotte's last choice as a hiding place. Enclosed spaces, *dark* enclosed spaces, were one of her terrors. Small rooms often made breathing difficult for her and, normally, when faced with a small room without a window, she simply wouldn't enter. For the moment, however, both the reality of her situation and the irony of it were pushed to the back of her mind. Not only was she in a closet, she was almost glad to be there — even if the size of her bustle, together with the large hat and parasol, made the dark space so cramped she couldn't turn around. Right now, her fear of being caught was far more urgent than her claustrophobia.

Not that she had been doing anything illegal. Well, perhaps technically she had. In truth, more than technically, it really *was* illegal. She had just broken into the private office of Algernon Methuen. Granted, if Algernon were to get up from his desk to get the bottle of sherry she knew was hidden somewhere here in the darkness with her — it was one of his secret habits — Charlotte was more likely to suffer supreme embarrassment than arrest. On the one hand, Algernon Methuen was not likely to bring about the arrest of Charlotte Riston-Winters, currently his top-selling author. But, on the other, how many established British publishers find one of their authors in an office closet? On a Sunday morning?

What was so upsetting was that Charlotte had planned it all ever so carefully. First, she had manipulated her appointment for the initial contract discussion so that she had been Algernon's last visitor the day before. Then she'd contrived to be late, and stalled all through the meeting so that the outer offices would be empty when she left. There was even an unplanned bonus when Algernon gave his personal secretary permission to go home for the day. Uncharacteristic for the old boy — almost shocking — for that meant he was left alone with a woman. Right on the edge of propriety, but in a way it reinforced something she had suspected all along: that he saw her as an author first and fore-most, and only incidentally as a woman. In any case, that part of the plan had worked perfectly, for Algernon had left the blank contract and his negotiating figures on the desk.

Then this morning . . . Charlotte had thought everything through. She had dressed conservatively to avoid attracting atten-tion. She hadn't worn any scent, for it might linger in the air. She knew the building would be empty but she'd left her town house and walked to the Clarendon, where they had those new tele-phones, and placed a call to Algernon's office. He liked new gadgets, and was one of the first in London to have one. A few minutes later, riding in the back of the hansom, Charlotte had a chill when she realized she had not thought about what she would do if he had actually answered. But he hadn't, so she could move ahead.

The cab had let her out on Fleet Street, well down from Fetter Lane, and she'd walked from there. No one had been on the street except for a crossing-boy and he hadn't looked up, his eyes fixed instead on the piles of horse dung he was being paid to clean up. Getting into the building was simple, as was getting into Algernon's office. From that point, things had proceeded almost like a plot in one of her novels. She'd settled into the old boy's big leather chair and taken her time paging through the contract.

What she saw made her squirm with annoyance. The initial offer yesterday was less than half what the accompanying figures showed Methuen could easily afford for her new book! But what made her truly burn was the note from the company solicitor. It was typewritten — trust *him* to use one of those vile new inventions! — and its contents advised Algernon: "Whilst Riston-Winters has enjoyed some success, she has unreasonable expectations for a woman, and the company should not be expected to establish a precedent by paying her the same royalty rate it pays to male authors."

The note had so infuriated Charlotte that the clumping sound of footsteps had almost reached the office door before she realized it. The sound was familiar. Algernon himself. The closet — thank heavens she knew about it — was the only refuge!

That was only seconds ago. Now, in the darkness of the closet, Charlotte willed her heartbeat to slow down to normal. She listened to the clumps cross the office, and heard Algernon settle into the chair. If her luck held, he would leave without ever knowing anyone was in the office. But before that could happen, there were two crisis points to get past, one immediate, and one that would become a problem in five minutes, maybe even less.

 Within five minutes, Charlotte's claustrophobia is bound to become active and may cause her to be discovered. That's one of the two crisis points. What is the immediate one?

FILE # 15

A Hero Mistreated?

February 17, 1961

Chesley McInerney, Esq.
Assistant Deputy Minister
Department of Pensions
Veterans Affairs Canada

Dear Mr. McInerney,

Further to our telephone conversation of February 9,
I am writing in regard to unpaid pension supplements due
the late Sergeant-Major Randall Moulton Foster, D.S.O.,
(b. Moltke, Ontario, August 2, 1880; d. Armentières,
France, December 12, 1915).

To support this petition, I make reference to Section IV
(b) (i, ii) of the Veterans Supplementary Pension Act, 1919:

> i: In addition to the regular pension paid to veterans of
> the Canadian Forces, the Government of Canada shall
> pay an annual supplement, the amount to be one-fifth

(1/5) of the base pension, to any veteran decorated for bravery on two or more separate occasions while on front-line service.

ii: The benefit referred to in IV (b) (i) shall be paid to a surviving spouse for the lifetime of said spouse.

Randall Foster served with the 2nd (Special Service) Battalion, Royal Canadian Regiment, from October 1899 to February 1901, and saw active front-line service during the conflict in South Africa. He also served with the First Canadian Division starting in September 1914 and saw active front-line service in Belgium and France from March 1915 until his death later that year. A pension, as stipulated by the Act of 1919, was duly paid to Gilbertha Foster, surviving spouse of Randall, until her death in July 1960. However, Mrs. Foster was also eligible for the annual supplement as outlined in Section IV (b), because her husband was decorated twice. For acts of bravery at Paardeburg (Dec 10–15, 1899), Sergeant-Major Foster received the Distinguished Service Order. This is verified in the record. Information attached to this petition, but missing from the record until now, shows that he received the Military Cross during World War I.

It is well established that the resistance of the Canadian infantry was largely responsible for preventing a major enemy breakthrough during the now famous gas attack at Ypres on April 22, 1915 (Second Battle of Ypres). According to battlefield accounts of the attack, Sgt.-Maj. Foster, along with 2nd Lieutenant, J. Peter Speight, were the only members of their platoon to survive, and the attached letter, sent May 15, 1923, to Gilbertha Foster from 2nd Lt. (now Major) Speight, shows that Sgt.-Maj. Foster was decorated at Ypres that day. This letter was found in Mrs. Foster's personal effects after her death last July. I quote two paragraphs:

When the relief force finally arrived, General Anthony told Sgt.-Maj. Foster that he would be awarded the Military Cross and put this on a dispatch I was to take personally to Haig's headquarters. But I was seriously wounded by the same artillery barrage that killed Anthony only an hour or so later.

I hope you can forgive me, Mrs. Foster, but not until a reunion of World War I veterans last month did I learn that Anthony's dispatch was never delivered.

As you indicated in our telephone conversation, there is precedent for posthumous awarding of military decorations on the basis of evidence such as this, and I am requesting, therefore, that the award of Military Cross go forward for Sergeant-Major Foster and that the supplement referred to in IV (b) be paid to Gilbertha Foster's estate.

Respectfully,

Harriet Blowes

February 25, 1961
Memo from C. McInerney to B.V. Donaldson,
re attached petition:

The fraud is pretty obvious. Do I call in the RCMP? Foster was KIA so it could be embarrassing. Any suggestions?

27/02/61
Donaldson to McInerney:

Go easy. Phone her and see if she'll withdraw the petition so we don't have to expose her publicly.

 What is the "pretty obvious fraud" in Harriet (Foster) Blowes's petition?

FILE # **16**

Concentrating the Search

Vic Krafchek took a deep breath and eased down on one knee to study the back seat of the Lincoln Town Car where Willie "The Mastodon" Smith had stopped a bullet with his head. Willie was in the center, one huge foot in each floor well on either side of the "hump." Except for the hole in his left temple and the little rivulets of blood that ran back over his ear to the back of his shaved head, he looked quite comfortable.

His mouth hung open, perhaps a bit more than normal, revealing the pair of extremely long and slightly curved upper canines that gave him his nickname. Each hand lay gently on his knees, and his head rested back against the top of the seat as though he were just catching forty winks. Nonetheless, Willie was dead, and Vic Krafchek — the newly appointed chief of detectives — had caught the call.

Usually at times like this, Vic would complain that, in a city with over four hundred murders a year, he always seemed to get the tough ones. And this was a tough one all right. Even a rookie cop on a first call could tell that Willie's death was a gangland execution, and, for any number of reasons, murders of this kind were among the hardest to solve. Most of the time, the hits were professional, with few clues to follow. They almost always took place, as this one did, in rundown or abandoned industrial areas where witnesses, if there were any, suffered from terrible eyesight and even worse memory. And then there was the unspoken but implicitly acknowledged lack of enthusiasm on the part of the police in these cases. If these guys wanted to bump each other off, well . . .

But Vic wasn't complaining this time. To begin with, there really was no one to complain to, now that he was the chief. Besides, there were too many other pressures right now to even think about grumbling. One was the media. They weren't here yet, but they would be soon. A patrolman had discovered the car around 4:00 a.m. and called it in. Even at that time of the morning there were reporters roving around with their scanners on. They liked stuff like this. Willie's murder would make good copy, so Vic knew he'd have to go all out.

Going all out was another pressure. The homicide department, like the rest of the force — indeed, the whole city — was decimated by an epidemic of the flu. Even if he pulled in officers from traffic and bunko and vice or whatever, Vic knew he still didn't have the resources to follow standard procedure on this one. Standard procedure involved a thorough canvass of the area right away. Willie had been shot with a small caliber gun — likely a .22, since there was no exit wound. Chances were a search just might turn up the gun. And although the odds of rousting a cooperative witness were slim, you just never knew.

Actually, that was another pressure: the witness thing. One of the first changes Vic had instituted after his promotion was to bring payoffs into the open. Every beat cop, every detective had informants. Sometimes they were paid with favors, sometimes with seized goods that mysteriously disappeared from lockup inventory, but most of the time they were paid with the police department's under-the-counter slush fund. What Vic had done was to make it known publicly that informants could expect to receive cash. Now he had to prove that the system would work. He had to show that, after the initial flood of informants that would inevitably swarm out of the gutters looking for a quick buck, the system would settle back into a workable — and accountable — one. The problem was, it was still early days, and his opponents were still waiting for the proof.

The fact that they just might be right nagged at Vic. And right here in front of him was a possible example. The patrolman who'd found Willie had had a street dweller in tow when Vic first arrived on the scene. Behind his unkempt hair and knockout breath, the wino claimed he'd heard a shot right here where the car was parked, and that two men had gotten out and run to the subway entrance across the street. Trouble was, a second officer had driven in with an informant too, another of the many cardboard-box residents who populated the area. This one's story was that he'd seen Willie get into the Town Car six blocks away, with two men; then he'd heard a shot and the car had taken off in this direction.

Vic got up off his knee. There were only enough officers to canvass one of the two areas right away, and staring at Willie's body wasn't going to help him pick the right one. Or was it?

 How can Willie's body help Vic decide which of the two informants is probably the best bet?

FILE # 17

Don't Get Caught
Speeding in Polk County!

"These aren't regulation gloves." Tony Jerome tossed first one, then a second pair of long black gauntlets onto the table. Then he picked one up again and sniffed it. "Leather though," he said with authority. "Genuine."

Fran Doublet tried to hold back the edge of sarcasm that always crept into her voice whenever she discussed evidence with the kidnap team's premier chauvinist. She didn't succeed.

"Since when did gloves become regulated items?" In spite of herself, she lifted her nose at him, just a touch. No matter how sincere her resolve not to, Fran could never resist the opportunity for a jab. She leaned over the table and poked at the pile on it with her pen.

"Or mace holders? Or these sunglasses? Both pairs the same, but *regulation*? And look!" She picked up an ammunition clip. "Speed loaders! When was the last time you saw equipment like this in a rural county police force? Especially one like Polk County!"

Tony Jerome wasn't easy to move. "You sure those have been cleared for prints?" he replied, without a change of expression.

Fran reddened. Not at the response but at the attitude. They both knew that the two uniforms lying on the table in front of them, along with all the accompanying police paraphernalia, had been gone over thoroughly by forensics. Nothing whatever had been found. The kidnappers in this case were pros.

"What I meant, *Agent* Jerome," Fran gave in completely to her impulses. She outranked Tony Jerome, but only in moments of extreme frustration did she let herself remind him. "What I meant was that accessories vary from police force to police force. When you have motorcycle people on the road, what gloves they wear depends on what the purchasing department gets for them. Unless they buy their own, and who does that? The same thing is true for utility belts, boots, helmets . . ." With her pen, she drummed the two white helmets on the table using far more energy than she intended to. "Other things, the extra bits, the personal preferences, the comfort stuff, they're personal buys, so generally they get what they want and what they can afford. As long as it's not something outrageous. After all, those gloves aren't pink now, are they?"

Tony looked at her directly for the first time, his face a mask as he spoke. "I saw a little coffee counter in a room just behind the sergeant's desk. I need a coffee. Would you like one? And maybe something to nibble if I can find it? It's been a while since lunch."

Fran was taken by surprise. Could the offer be his way of apologizing? Or just maybe an acknowledgement that no matter what her gender, her considerably greater experience — not to mention her past successes — with the FBI's kidnap response team gave her an implicit right to lead the investigation?

"Uh . . . thanks." She came close to a stutter but recovered fast. "Just a touch of milk, please, if they've got it. Oh, and ask the sergeant if that interview room is ready yet."

The young man turned to the door, offering a half-salute with two fingers of one hand, a gesture that fell precisely at the midpoint between smugness and respect.

"A touch of milk. Interview room. Oh . . ." he paused at the door. "What do you make of the trouser stripes? Not what they wear on Polk County uniforms, is it?" He closed the door softly.

A single glance confirmed for Fran that she'd missed the stripes completely. This time she turned beet-red. And there was no relief in knowing that Tony Jerome couldn't see it. He knew darn well that in all the flurry and hyperactivity that inevitably occurs at the front end of a kidnapping investigation, she hadn't picked up on the stripes. Not that it mattered all that much by now. By now they knew for sure that the cops who'd taken off with Wendel Chabot Jr. were not cops at all. Nor had it been hard to figure that out. But still, she'd missed the stripes. And Tony knew it.

The regulation uniforms of the Polk County Sheriff's Department had a full-length red stripe on the outside of each trouser leg. It was a relatively narrow stripe, but unique in that the edges were serged, making them thicker, so that even though the material was all the same color, the effect was almost, but not quite, one of three stripes. It was a tiny design quirk, and Fran could almost hear some weenie in the Polk County Clerk's Department saying "Hey, why not!" when the time had come to re-style the county's police uniforms. The trousers she was looking at right now had duplicated the color exactly, and the width, but the serging along the borders wasn't there.

Everything else was, though, most especially the shoulder patches that clearly identified officers of the Polk County Sheriff's Department. In fact, other than the stripes, there was nothing about the uniforms that would suggest that the two men who'd stopped Wendel Chabot's limousine were anything but the genuine item. No wonder Chabot's personal driver/bodyguard had pulled over without protest. Fran acknowledged to herself, and not for the first time either, that she'd have done precisely the same thing.

Earlier that day, somewhere between 1030 hrs. and 1100 hrs., as the Costas County deputy had reported to her, Wendel Chabot Jr.'s mid-morning nap in the back of his stretch limo had been interrupted on a stretch of rural highway by what appeared to be two Polk County officers on motorcycles. The driver had slowed and then stopped on the shoulder, expecting a reprimand, maybe even a citation, for speeding. What he got instead was the barrel of a gun behind his ear. He was immediately blindfolded and tied up. The "officers" put a note into his pocket that read: START GETTING CASH — YOU'LL HEAR FROM US, then rolled him into the ditch beside the road and drove away with the limousine, Chabot inside.

He'd worked his way loose in only a few moments, in time to flag down the first car to come along. It was driven by a teenager who accepted twenty bucks to drive him back over the state line into Costas County where he'd called the sheriff's office. Suspicion of kidnapping and the crossing of state lines had brought in the FBI, hence Fran and Tony's involvement. By the time the two arrived at the Costas County sheriff's office in the mid-afternoon, the Polk County uniforms had been found in some bushes near the kidnap site.

"Here's your coffee."

Fran hadn't even heard Tony come in.

"I think the milk's OK. It's one of *those* squad room kitchens. There were cookies, but you wouldn't want them. And the interview room's ready. Bodyguard's in it, waiting."

"Good. Let's go," Fran replied immediately. She was glad to get moving. "Tony," she said as they walked down the hall, "the trouser stripes . . . oh . . . uh . . . thanks, the coffee's fine . . . the stripes. That was good. Don't know how I missed that."

Tony Jerome dismissed the compliment with a small wave. Fran couldn't help notice it was a salute again.

"No big deal," he said, "the stripes, I mean. But they're pretty good confirmation the kidnappers didn't get the uniforms from the Polk department. 'Least they're not in cahoots on this thing."

"Not unless they want us to think that way!" Fran felt a little better after that one for Tony's expression indicated he hadn't yet thought of the possibility. Before he could say anything, however, she went on, all business now. "OK, you question this — what's his name again? — yeah, Savage. Eustis Savage. Heck of a name! I'll stay on the other side of the glass. Go easy on him. For now he's just a witness. All you do is go over the same ground the Costas deputy did. See if his story changes. Boy, I like that name!"

Eustis Savage's shape was as unusual as his name. It was a kindergarten construction, a rectangular block, with a small square on top, set ever so slightly askew. The arms, the hands and feet, even the slab-like face, all looked like a five-year-old's design. Yet the man's speech had such an elevated correctness that, to Fran, he came across like an Oxford don.

"No, I was not alarmed," Fran watched him reply to Tony. "After all, they were policemen . . . well rather, they *looked* the way policemen always seem to look on highway patrol. And I had indeed been accelerating quite beyond the posted limit. That was at Mr. Chabot's insistence, by the bye."

"Tell us again," Tony was trying to sound casual, "why you paid that kid to drive you here to Costas."

"Surely, to compensate the young man was not unreasonable. After all, he had to go well out of his way. And why this county? Costas? To be frank, I wasn't sure of its name, but having attended to the road signs, I knew it was over the state line, and that, most importantly, it wasn't Polk County. Wouldn't you agree that my experience gave me reason to doubt the integrity of Polk County officers?"

"So you knew they were Polk. You saw their shoulder patches?"

"Only a glance, but that was sufficient."

"But in your statement to the Costas County deputy, you said they held a gun to your head and wouldn't let you turn around."

"That's correct, Agent Jerome."

Fran suppressed a chuckle. Eustis Savage was managing Tony like a student who'd come for extra help after class.

"However, I'm sure you appreciate that often, in moments of high drama, one's powers of concentration are enhanced. Not only could I read the shoulder patch — that was not terribly difficult, by the bye — but I noted the type of motorcycle: Harley-Davidson '74. 'Goobers,' I believe they're called in the parlance of aficionados."

This time Fran laughed out loud. The Costas deputy who did the first interview was an utter clod. He must have been thrilled by "parlance of aficionados."

"And, as careful as they were, I was still able to use the side mirror if only for a few seconds. Enough on a bright day like today to see the reddish moustache on one of the alleged officers, and his brown eyes. He had big, rather pouty lips, too."

Tony was drawing a long breath for his next question when Fran stuck her head in the door.

"Tony, may I speak to you out in the hall, please?" Her tone had an urgency that told him not to waste time arguing.

"No more," she said to him seconds later, "not until we Mirandize him. He's a suspect now, and this guy for sure'll want a lawyer. Stay here till I call this in!"

She spun on her heel and walked quickly down the hall toward a bank of telephones. Too quickly to see and enjoy the look of complete bewilderment on Tony's face.

 Why has Eustis Savage become a suspect in the kidnapping (if it is a kidnapping now)? What has Fran picked up that Tony has apparently missed?

FILE # 18

The Unseen Hijacker

Arthur Glass spoke first. "Only one of the flight attendants got a good look at him. Tawnee Burke. She was the one he took into the restroom with him. And she didn't see much because her back was toward him the whole time. The others have a vague recollection — white male, clean-shaven, black or dark blue baseball cap, medium height and size, medium everything. Flight was just half full and he sat by himself near the back. So far we don't have a single passenger who remembers anything about him."

He paused, but the others kept looking at him, so he carried on. "According to the manifest, the hijacker's name is George Smith."

There were rueful smiles at the table.

"What happens is, everything on the flight is normal until they're about thirty minutes from landing at Tucson. Burke is by herself at the back when he grabs her by the hair. Presses something sharp into her neck. Says she's sure it was a knife but she never actually saw it. He makes her grab the intercom beside the door and backs the two of them into the restroom."

Glass turned his hand to Veronica Page in an "over to you" gesture but then added, "Oh, one thing." He sat forward. "Burke confirms the height. She's five-seven and the guy's about the same. And she's also sure about this: He had brown eyes, but she saw a blue edge. Like maybe he was wearing colored contacts."

Veronica Page looked at Glass intently. When it was obvious he was finished, she spoke. "The pilot is setting up for approach into Tucson when Burke calls him on the intercom. Tells him a hijacker — well, a *passenger* — has her in the restroom. He's got a knife on her neck, and he's showing her two sticks of dynamite."

"How'd he ever get *dynamite* past security?" Moe Gupta jumped in on behalf of the rest.

"You have to ask?" Page looked at him.

There were knowing nods from the group before she continued. "Now the thing about the dynamite — she . . . er . . . Burke . . . describes it to the pilot and he relays it to the marshals in Denver — they're in on it right away. Seems all the wiring is right, the caps and detonator and so on, but what really scares them is that she says it looks *wet*. Now that can only mean one thing: it's old and it's sweating. Which makes it very unstable."

"The top explosives guy in Denver," Victor Glass broke in. "This guy tells the pilot that what she's describing has to be the real thing. You just can't fake something like that."

Page took up again. "Yeah, so now Burke tells the pilot the guy wants to divert to Phoenix, so he gets clearance to land at Sky Harbor there."

"Did the 'jacker ever talk to the pilot directly?" It was Moe Gupta again.

"No," Page answered. "Burke says she tried to get the guy to talk, but he only spoke when he gave instructions. He did keep muttering something over and over, though. Like a chant in a foreign language. She's trying to repeat it for the marshals right now. Anyway, the pilot gets on the blower, tells the passengers they're diverting to Phoenix because Tucson is closed. Then Burke calls forward again. What he wants is $250,000 in used fifties in an overnight bag."

Arthur Glass leaned forward. "Kind of piddly, isn't it? Two hundred and fifty grand? For a hijack?"

Page shook her head. "Not if you're going to jump with it. Bulk and weight. He also asked for a parachute, a sports model." She was allowing herself to get just a bit excited. Page, it seemed, had more than a little respect for the hijacker. "And the time factor too. See . . . the airline's only got half an hour or so. If it was a million, they'd need more time to get it together. And there might be time to mark it, or record serial numbers. The parachute, too. Really no time to doctor it somehow, like with maybe a tracking device or something."

Moe Gupta now took over. "The money and the 'chute are to be taken to Goodyear . . ."

"Goodyear!" The man at the head of the table spoke for the very first time.

"Yes, Phoenix Goodyear Airport!" Gupta replied. "At the last minute, the pilot is told to divert from Sky Harbor to Goodyear. There's only one runway there that can take a 727. This guy knew his stuff." He waited for comment. When none came, he continued.

"Switching airports made the time really tight. The people on the ground really had to scramble to get to Goodyear. Anyway, the pilot puts 'er down there, and the passengers get off and so do all the attendants except Burke. Only her and the cockpit crew left.

"Goes fast from here. The money and the 'chute are taken back to the restroom. Two of our guys do this and then get off. Then the pilot is told to take off and fly to Tucson. Two hundred knots at 2500 feet. Which he does. Burke then is told to go up into the cockpit, and somewhere over Arizona the 'jacker goes out a rear emergency door."

When the man at the head of the table frowned, Gupta added quickly, "No real risk of depressurization at 2500 feet. And, I'm tellin' ya, this guy did his homework — or else he's an airline insider. A 727 is about the only aircraft you could do this with. Open up like that, I mean. Couldn't do it in an airbus or a 747 or whatever."

Arthur Glass chimed in again. "Radar followed the plane, of

course, but there was no pickup on anyone jumping. That's iffy anyway, a parachute. And, so far, there's nothing unusual on the ground between Phoenix and Tucson. Big-time search, but it's turned up absolute zip. Same with the search of the plane, so he definitely got away with the money."

At the head of the table, the man who had spoken only once now leaned forward and looked at each of the others in turn. "What did you turn up when you searched Burke's personal effects?" he asked.

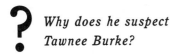

Why does he suspect
Tawnee Burke?

FILE # 19

A Rash of Break-ins

19623 The Old Mill Road: 1:15 p.m.
Tiffany Stock is alone at home, gardening.

It was just after lunch when Tiffany Stock saw the police car come into the driveway. She was standing near the back of the property where the driveway curved, where she'd put in the bed of salvia and dusty miller earlier in the spring. The car drove in slowly and the rack of roof lights was still, so there was no indication of an emergency. Yet she couldn't help feeling a deep sense of unease. Ed, her husband, was at work. Had something happened to him? She had spoken to him not more than an hour ago. Reminded him that it was parents' invitation night at St. Bart's. The kids! Not another bus accident! Couldn't be! Not at 1:00! And she'd have heard by now if something had gone amiss this morning. What if it was — she couldn't finish the thought. The very idea of guns or any weapon in her kids' school was beyond her.

That kind of speculation had made her truly nervous by the time the car rolled up to her. Rather than look at the man behind the wheel, she stared at the hood ornament on the white Crown

Victoria, watching it lead the vehicle to where she stood. The man who got out was muscular and lanky. To Tiffany he seemed to unfold from the front seat.

"Beautiful property," he said. "Are you the gardener, or do you have a service?"

The greeting didn't register with Tiffany at first. It took more than a few seconds for her to realize the officer wasn't offering some version of, "I'm sorry, Mrs. Stock, but . . ."

"No. I mean, yes!" she finally blurted. "I mean it's mostly me. It's a hobby."

"Well, you certainly have the touch." He stepped toward her and offered his hand. "P.C. Johnson."

"Er . . . Stock. Tiffany Stock." She held out her hand in response but then suddenly became aware it held a trowel.

The officer smiled. "Sorry to disturb you but we're spending part of every shift this week visiting homes in the area. I'm sure you have heard about the recent rash of break-ins?"

She hadn't, but nodded yes anyway.

"So we're trying to contact as many homeowners as we can. Beautiful homes like yours can be a target. We just want you to be alert to the problem, and ask that you take some precautions."

Relief and gratitude flooded through her entire body. Everybody was safe. "Would you . . . would you . . ." She didn't know what to say and then heard herself asking, "Would you like some tea? It would just be a minute."

"That's very kind," he replied, "but as you can see I'm on duty. I'd appreciate a glass of water though. It's a warm day."

He followed Tiffany back up the driveway to the side entrance of the house.

"Lovely home. I'm sure you and your family . . . by the way, your television set there." The side entrance opened to Tiffany's sunroom, and that, in turn, led to a large den, where a large-screen television set took up space beside a set of patio doors. "That's the type of thing you should have security for. Do you know the serial number of the set? Or do you have a means of tracing it?"

Tiffany had returned with a glass of ice water. She shook her head weakly.

"Well, it's advisable." He paused to drink the water. "Especially in a nice place like this."

He handed back the glass and, after another minute or so of cautioning her about security, excused himself and returned to the car. Tiffany watched him back out of the driveway and then realized she had been carrying the trowel the whole time.

19623 The Old Mill Road: 7:15 p.m.
The Stock family is exiting the driveway en route to St. Bart's.

Ed had been late getting home. He'd only had time to gulp part of a plate of warmed-up lasagna and brush his teeth before getting into the car with Tiffany and the kids.

". . . and there I was," Tiffany was saying, laughing at herself. She was finishing up her account of the officer's visit earlier that day. "I was holding the trowel the whole time! Even at that I don't think I'd have picked up on it, except that while he was backing out I had this itchy nose. And suddenly I felt the trowel on my face!"

Tiffany began to laugh harder as the image of scratching her face with a garden trowel hit home. She didn't notice that Ed was frowning until she felt the car turn sharply left.

"Ed!" she exclaimed. "Where are you going? St. Bart's is that way!"

"Yes, and the police station is this way," he replied. "What did you say his name was? Johnson? If you ask me, our house was cased this afternoon. If they don't have a Johnson out of this station, we're going home right away."

 Why does Ed Stock suspect that P.C. Johnson may not be a P.C. (police constable) at all, and that their house was being "cased"?

FILE # 20

Random Shots
by the River

Sheriff Orson "Mack" MacTier usually looked over the top of his glasses whenever he spoke while sitting at his desk. It spared him the discomfort of bending at the neck to look up. Mack's uniforms had been far too tight for some time now but, rather than visit a tailor or a gym, he'd simply adapted his posture.

"Somebody's gotta go out to the Greevelys," the sheriff was saying to his newest deputy, "and you got the short straw."

The young officer standing just inside the doorway of Mack's stuffy office nodded his head once and waited for more. He knew about the situation — it was one of those incidents his wife had taken to calling "country crimes" after they'd moved here — but the significance of the Greevelys was something new to him, so he waited for more.

And Mack had more. "The Greevely place is the first one on the left after the bridge. When you turn off Route 40 onto Cottonwood Road — mind, you're going south — there's two farms, both on the left. Nothin' on the right but swamp. Then comes the river flat where the kids had the campfire. The Snider place is in back of the flat. Can't see it from the road, but that's no matter to you for now. Right after the flat is the bridge, and after the bridge is the Greevelys."

The young deputy nodded again. This time he shifted a bit toward the door. It appeared Mack might be finished, but just in case . . .

The type of "country crime" that may or may not have involved the Greevelys, whoever they were — likely another oddball local family that he would have to get to know sooner or later — was something Deputy Tim Rodney had never encountered in his three years on the force in St. Louis. Last night, some time before midnight, out on the "river flat," a local term for a small flood plain, a group of about a half dozen youngsters, maybe ten to twelve years old, had gathered with some homemade wine that one of them had conveniently lifted from his father's cellar. Like many other kids in Ayton County with not enough to do, they biked out to the flat and lit a fire. This was not a bush party. Tim had run into his first of those the previous week: almost a hundred teenagers, roaring drunk around an even more roaring bonfire.

This was just a bunch of bored kids who, most of the time, would have sat around their campfire until one or two of them got sick enough on the wine to brag about it at the local poolroom on the weekend, and then would have gotten on their bikes and gone home. But several of them had brought their .22s. With the wine and the boredom and the darkness, the rifles made a potent mix.

About 11:30 p.m., at the farms nearest the river flat, shots were heard. Again, no big deal here in the county, even that late at night. But there were a lot of shots, and eventually first one bullet, then several more, went through the front windows at the Snider place. Fortunately, no one was hurt, but Mack was treating the situation with — in Tim's limited experience thus far — uncharacteristic seriousness.

Mack was not finished. "Go easy there. With the Greevelys, I mean." Mack had lifted his head and was looking through his glasses, so Tim knew the advice was serious. "You've only been here a month, but you'll get to know 'em more 'n you want. What you do is, you ask 'em what they heard and so on, but they got a kid about the right age. Their youngest one. Name's Lawson. We know there were at least six kids there at the flat and at least three of 'em had guns. I'd bet our shiny new patrol car out there that young Lawson's one of 'em. Him and me, we've talked before, number of times. I'm figurin' if he's one of 'em, he'll have a few things to say to me 'bout what happened. Owes me, that boy."

The Greevely place was everything Tim had expected it to be. He drove down the potholed lane carefully, for the long grass that grew between the wheel tracks hid large rocks. He was unable to distinguish the house from the barn and other ramshackle outbuildings until he got right up to it. The customary dogs of dubious ancestry set up an immediate howl the minute he drove in, but Tim had learned by now that their noise was usually bluff, and that, on these farms, dogs served as doorbells. But he regarded with far more caution the small gaggle of geese that waited until the last second before getting out of his way. Even though spring was almost over, the gander leading the troop might still have seasonal randiness, and he knew from experience that police uniforms were poor protection from gander bites. He also knew that he had to get past the gander and the dogs and around to the back door. Front entrances in the typical home out here had little more than symbolic purpose.

"Mrs. Greevely?" he said to the shadowy figure that answered his knock by opening the door just a crack. "My name's Rodney, Deputy Rodney."

The door opened wider. "Never seen you before. Must be one a' the new ones."

She was a thin woman with no particularly outstanding features except an aspect of total weariness.

"Are you Mrs. Greevely?" Tim repeated.

She didn't answer, but instead focused on the porch steps behind him. Tim looked around to see the gander pacing back and forth at the bottom step. Behind him, three dogs sat eyeing

Tim with a neutral gaze. A fourth, then a fifth dog appeared at the corner of the house.

"Better come in," the woman said, and led him into a narrow hallway.

On either side of him, Tim was aware of at least a dozen woolen plaid overshirts, a standard spring and fall uniform out here on the river farms. Each hung separately on nails tapped into the top of the wainscot. What impressed him was the number. Obviously, there were quite a few Greevelys.

"Men are in the barn," the woman said, when she saw him looking at the shirts. "Chores," she added, as though that explained why such an apparently large roster was absent.

Tim cleared his throat. "I have a few questions about the Snider place getting shot up last night."

Her eyebrows lifted. "Don't know nothin' 'bout the Sniders. Heard shots last night, though. Figured you was gonna ask 'bout that."

"You heard the shots then?" Tim said. "Do you recall what time?"

She shifted her weight from one foot to the other.

"Don't pay much 'tention to gunfire 'round here, y'know," she said. "But there was quite a lotta shootin'." She paused and shifted yet again. "Had to be after eleven. Archie, him and Lawson was watchin' Jay Leno. Comes on after eleven, don't it? I was in bed, but Archie, he's got the TV on so loud all the time. That's when I heard the shots."

Tim made himself go slow and be casual.

"Lawson's your youngest, right?" he said.

"Be twelve come the fall."

"This one his?" Tim picked up a smaller plaid shirt from the row.

"Yeah." She frowned. "Here now, what you gonna do with it?"

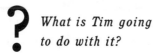 *What is Tim going to do with it?*

An Eye for Details

From the doorway, Breen Morris swept the office slowly from left to right with careful, discerning eyes. It was a habit of hers on suspected homicide calls: Get the big picture first, then go for the details. The big picture, in this case, appeared to be the aftermath of a small celebration in a very expensively decorated office on what was probably the most expensive floor of an extremely expensive building. Clients didn't show up here expecting a discount, that was for sure.

As for the details . . . the most striking detail was a pair of feet Breen could see sticking out from behind one corner of the desk. They were heels-up, toes-down in shiny, black leather wingtips. Size 11, she surmised, and from this angle, she was betting on triple-wide. Breen had worked in a shoe store in college. Unfortunately for the man wearing them, neither the quality nor the size of the shoes mattered any more. He was dead.

Breen stepped forward to the desk. The next detail to attract her attention was a half-empty bottle of champagne resting in a sterling silver bucket. The label on the bottle confirmed an assumption: Dom Perignon, it declared, in an arrogant Gothic script. She stared at the tiny beads of condensation that rimmed the ornate letters. Of course it would be the best stuff. Breen wouldn't have been surprised to hear that the ghost of the old Dom himself had been hired to pour.

She leaned close to the bottle and sniffed at the top of the neck. Nothing unusual, she thought. Other than the fact that it was pricey booze, Breen didn't really know much about champagne. To her, it smelled just like any other wine. The contents of the bottle, nevertheless, were another detail, this one to be set aside for analysis. The forensics people would have to run tests. On the stuff left in the two glasses, too. They were on a small table in the corner; she'd noted that while standing in the doorway. One glass, the empty one, stood precisely in the middle of a coaster. The other, half full, leaned precariously to the left, because whoever set it down had partially missed the coaster.

Above the table a huge window offered an unobstructed view of the lake to the west. Breen turned her gaze that way. It was an impressive sight. Looking at the lip of the horizon, she could see the last sliver of the setting sun, and she shook her head at the realization that, for the people down on the street, the sun was already gone for the day. Wonder what the old Dom would think of that, she mused. She stepped closer to the window, then stopped abruptly. On the other side of the desk was a detail she had not seen from the doorway. Quite possibly an important one.

Lying on the floor was an irregular greenish slab, about the size and general shape of a dinner plate, and about as thick as a small paperback. It looked like something cut from a piece of rock, then ground and polished smooth on two sides. There was a small black box on the smooth side Breen could see, in the center, with a battery in it. Very carefully, she knelt on one knee and using only her gloved hand, lifted the slab at one edge and turned it to get a look at the other side. It was a clock. The numbers, large Arabic numbers, were made of polished, fine brass. The minute and hour hands were long and delicate. Both of them were bent. Breen watched the long, thin second hand, waiting for it to move. It didn't. It couldn't, because one end was jammed into the circle that made the number 9. The clock had stopped at 5:29. When it fell off its stand on the desk, she wondered?

"Malachite." A voice came from the doorway.

Breen realized she had totally forgotten the man in the outer office, the one who had called the police.

"The green stuff is called malachite." The voice continued. "It's a mineral they mine in Russia somewhere. He had a client there a couple of years ago. Won the case and the client gave him that clock. Keeps it on his desk. Claims it makes a good conversation piece."

"Don't come in!" Breen cautioned the owner of the voice. "Nobody comes in until forensics has gone over everything." She spoke with her back to the man in the doorway. She didn't want to look at him, partly because she now suspected him, and partly because she was embarrassed at forgetting he was still out there.

The speaker was the dead man's partner. As he had explained when Breen arrived, he and the firm's paralegal — their one secretary had been home sick all day — had left the office at about 5:00, leaving the victim to finish a drink with a client. The victim was to join the partner and the paralegal for dinner at 6:00 in a restaurant down at street level, before a night of work. When he hadn't shown up by 7:00, and didn't answer his phone, the partner got into the elevator and came up to investigate. Breen had answered the partner's anxious phone call an hour ago, at 7:10. Since that time, she had been trying to absorb the big picture and put the details in place, and, now, one of the details didn't fit.

 In the crime scene that Breen Morris is investigating, what is the detail that doesn't fit?

FILE #22

Nathan Greeley's Personal Effects

"**T**his pen here! The ballpoint! It's not on the list!" Shelley Budgell realized as soon as she'd said it that her voice had a finger-wagging tone, but this was the third time in the past few days that one of her squad had been careless. The reply she got from Officer Tabitha Van did nothing to make her feel better.

"It's just a cheap ballpoint pen, Sergeant," Van said. "What's it say on it — Denver Savings and Loan? Bet he doesn't even know he had it! You know how you put these things in your purse — or like, maybe your pocket if you're a guy — without even knowing."

"That makes absolutely no difference!" Shelley could sense her finger-wag changing to a pounding fist. "When you put someone in a cell, *everything* — absolutely everything the person has — gets inventoried. No exceptions. Nothing ignored. Not ever."

"I'm sorry, Sergeant Budgell. It won't happen again." Tabitha Van was so thoroughly humbled that Shelley felt a twinge of remorse. One of the toughest things about heading up a team was knowing when to kick butt and when to pat on the back. All police officers cut corners, she knew; she did it herself, but . . .

"Fine. Done with," she said. "Let's get on with it. They're bringing this Greeley character up in a few minutes."

"He's being discharged?" Tabitha Van seemed very surprised.

"Yes. Denver called about an hour ago. His alibi's solid. Apparently we've got it right here on an airline ticket. Oh, he was in Denver, all right, but only for a day or so before he came back home here to Detroit. Looks like he was thirty thousand feet in the air when his wife was shot."

"Actually . . . er . . . Sergeant, I meant the D&D charge."

"Yeah, the drunk and disorderly charge, too. It's being withdrawn." Shelley saw a chance now for a back pat. "You did everything right, Tab, when you picked him up. But he really wasn't causing much of a problem. You said yourself the clerk was probably overreacting. Besides, this is good old Detroit. We've got bigger problems than a guy who makes like he's going to pee in the back of a liquor store on Jefferson Avenue. Especially during the week before Christmas. You still get credit for the collar. It'll look good, too, with this Denver thing. The people downstairs will love you, for sure. I think the APB had slipped past them. Now let's get back to his personal effects."

The "Denver thing" had turned up when Tabitha had picked up Nathan Greeley in response to a drunk and disorderly complaint. Then, after she had brought Greeley in, she discovered an all-points bulletin on him, issued by the homicide department of the Denver police. He was wanted for questioning in the shooting murder of his estranged wife in that city two days before. As a result, what might have been a simple misdemeanor booking had turned into a possible serious crime, and Greeley had spent the night in a holding cell. This morning, however, Denver police had called to say they'd clearly established the time of the shooting at 4:00 p.m., and, at that precise moment, according to the airline ticket in Nathan Greeley's personal effects when he was arrested in Detroit, the man had been in seat 13A of United Airlines Flight 328.

"Um, Sergeant Budgell, I . . ." Tabitha was reluctant to bring up anything connected to the ballpoint pen, but she had little choice. "Should I enter the pen on the 'inventory in' list and check it now on the 'out' list."

"Might as well," Shelley replied, making an effort not to hammer home the issue again. "First, just call out the items. We'll check them as 'inventory out' and then both of us can sign off, so Greeley can have his stuff back."

"Right. Okay, top of the list is one plastic comb."

Shelley nodded.

"Cell phone. Nokia brand."

Another nod.

"Currency: one fifty-dollar bill, three twenties; thirty-five cents in coin. One hundred and sixty dollars in Canadian currency, all twenties."

The presence of Canadian money in the pockets of a Detroiter didn't even raise an eyebrow. The traffic flow across the border between Windsor, Ontario, and Detroit was like that of the small countries of central Europe. Tabitha turned to cough and then continued. "One pocket knife — I thought guys stopped carrying these things after the fifth grade!"

Shelley smiled and placed a check in the "out" column of the inventory. "Ours is not to reason why. The watch next?"

"Movado with a leather strap. This is a cool watch. What's it say? King . . . Kingmatic Classic. Bet that's worth a buck or two, unless it's a knockoff. It's slow by a good two hours. Was when I checked it in, too. One plastic entry card from the Hampton Inn. A leather wallet. Wallet's sealed, you notice?"

Tabitha was looking for praise. It was department policy to put a seal on wallets at the time of booking but the policy was regularly ignored.

Shelley gave her a thumbs up. "Is that the ticket?" she asked.

"Must be," the other officer replied. "I guess it's a very important personal effect now. At least to him."

Shelley frowned. "It's just listed here as 'ticket.' You didn't record any details?"

A touch of defiance crept into Tabitha Van's voice. Just a touch, but it was evident nonetheless. "When he was booked, it *was* just a ticket, a personal effect. It didn't become *evidence* until this morning."

Shelley backed off. "Guess that's true. Still, we'd better cover the bases. What's it say? Yeah. Here it is. User copy of a ticket, Detroit to Denver on United 1285 three days ago — out at 6:00 p.m. — and here's the return to Detroit the day before yesterday on United 328. Yeah, departure out of Denver is 3:40 p.m., so it looks like Nathan Greeley would have been in the air, all right, when his ex-wife took the hit." She leaned back and wrinkled her nose at the ticket. "That is, if it really was Greeley on that plane."

"What do you mean?" Tabitha Van slid to the edge of her chair. "You mean he might not have taken that flight?"

"Oh, someone took the flight all right; it's a used ticket. And it's Greeley's. Name's right there. But I think that after I call Denver back, they are going to want to see these personal effects and then take another look at his alibi.

 Something in Nathan Greeley's personal effects has made Sergeant Shelley Budgell suspicious of his alibi. What is that, and why does she think he may have been in Denver, after all, at the time of the shooting?

FILE # 23

Hunting the Blue Morpho

"**Y**ou're quite correct, Mrs. Larabee, Punta Blanca is a very primitive little village by North American standards. The people are very poor. There's a school, a store. A clinic but, unfortunately, no doctor. No telephone system, of course. Electricity only when there's gasoline for the generator. It's the very last town on the Pacific Coast before the Panamanian border. But keep in mind, your daughter is in Costa Rica. It's not like a lot of other Central American countries."

Salvador Rivas had lost track of how many times he had added the latter qualifier when he tried to explain his country to Americans. "There are no revolutions. My people are very friendly; we don't even have an army!"

Justina Larabee drew the four fingers of her right hand across her forehead, a regular habit of hers when she was stressed. "But my daughter . . . all her education and she's still such a . . . a . . . *naif*! It's bad enough this is her first time in jungle like that, but she — you could sell this child the Eiffel *Tower*! And that husband of hers, he's such an urban ninny. All he knows is how to find empty parking spaces!"

Salvador waited for more and, when it was not forthcoming,

tried another approach. "It's January, Mrs. Larabee, the dry season, so Punta Blanca is only about five to six hours from Golfito on the bush road."

"That's supposed to make me feel better?"

"Golfito is a major center. It's a port. There's a small airport. It has . . ."

"But no Blue Morpho butterflies!" For the first time, Mrs. Larabee seemed indignant rather than tearful. The man with her — Salvador assumed he was her husband — quietly placed a hand over hers.

"Blue Morpho butterflies? I don't understand." Salvador's temper was changing, just like Mrs. Larabee's. He was becoming annoyed and his voice showed it. "Of course there are Morphos around Golfito. Morphos can be found anywhere there's jungle in Central America. They are very important to us. My people have a belief that to see a Blue Morpho means good fortune will come to you."

"Forgive me, Mr. Rivas." Justina Larabee withdrew her hand from under her husband's and resumed stroking her forehead. "I didn't do a very good job of explaining. My daughter — Judith is her name — she is an entomologist. Rather, she *plans* to be. She'll start her doctoral studies next fall, you see. And what has happened is that when we were on vacation in Costa Rica last year on the . . . er . . . er . . . *dry* coast?"

"Yes. You probably flew into Liberia." Salvador was smiling again.

"That's right! That's right! Our resort was near there. And Judith, one day, in the village — no, it was more of a large town, a small city, Santa . . . Santa . . ."

"Santa Cruz?"

"That's right! That's right! In Santa Cruz, Judith met several others her age — you know how young people are — who told her that the principal mating ground for the Blue Morpho butterfly is near this Punta Blanca. And, of course, as soon as she heard that, she . . ."

Salvador Rivas nodded. As Costa Rica's *chargé d'affaires* in New

York he had more than a little experience with situations like this. The Blue Morpho mating grounds story was new to him but not improbable. Certainly this particular butterfly attracted a lot of attention and the coastal area below Golfito was all jungle. Perfect conditions for a mating ground, if there really was such a thing.

"I understand completely," he said, then tapped the phone. "As I said, Punta Blanca is quite out of the way, but one good thing, it's about the only place for hundreds of miles around where cell phones work. The satellite, you see. If she calls as planned . . ."

As though the matter were scripted, the telephone on Salvador Rivas's desk emitted an electronic buzz. Judith was right on schedule. Salvador punched on the speakerphone and then sat back, trying to withdraw himself from any of the personal elements of the conversation. It was only when the husband sat up abruptly that he began paying attention.

Judith was talking about Gustavo, the guide she and her husband had hired in Golfito. "He's got all this jungle experience, he's so cool! Kind of spooky but sort of Hemingway-like, not Stephen King. You know what I mean? Like, sometimes when we're in the rainforest, he walks right tight behind you, but you don't even know he's there! And he knows all about the Morph! Knew right away what we were talking about! You know, like, the mating ground? He's never been there when it's going on, but he knows where it is! Says it's about a day in on foot because the undergrowth's pretty thick. It's gonna be so cool!"

"Judy!" Mr. Larabee's very first word was startling.

"Daddy? Wow! Are you there? Daddy, this is so cool!"

"Judy!" Larabee *père* repeated. "I don't want you to do this!"

"Daddy, we've been all through this. I . . ."

"The guide, Judy. He's not what he says he is."

 What makes Judy Larabee's father think Gustavo is not what he claims to be?

FILE # 24

All the Pieces in Place

Morry Green could feel his heart slam right into his ribs. He'd been setting this thing up for months, yet he could scarcely believe that today — right *now!* — at this very moment! — all the pieces were falling into place. From where he hid in the trees across the road from the entrance to Amber Pines, Morry watched Wes, the gateman, leave the guard hut. It was 7:25 p.m. Perfect! Wes was leaving five minutes early for his break. Now Morry could scoot across the road, pass unseen through the unmanned security gate, and be inside his house in just under two minutes. He should know; he'd been timing this forever. Another two minutes for Naomi; two more to scatter some stuff around — to make it look like a break-in; one minute to tape the window and break it; and then two more to get back here into the park. Nine minutes. Add three for contingencies, and the magic number became twelve. Hard to believe. After years of marital agony, it would take only twelve minutes to find peace.

Morry took a deep breath, reached inside his coat, and set Sooki on the ground. The little shih-tzu shook herself and, true to form, stood silently, waiting for a tug on the leash. Sooki knew the routine as well as Morry and had long since accepted his sudden interest in taking her for walks. That had begun last June, about six months ago. Every night at 7:00 p.m., no matter what the weather — that was another important piece — Morry Green snapped on the little dog's leash, led her out the front door, and turned left toward the gate of Amber Pines, where he'd stop for a few minutes to chat with Wes, then cross the road into the park.

"Never misses, this guy," Wes once said to the security supervisor. "Comes out with that little dog right at 7:00. Goes across the road into the park, and then bang, right at 8:00 he comes back. I swear he'd go out in a tornado. I never seen him miss!"

All part of the plan. Morry needed to be seen going out at 7:00 and returning at 8:00. And it had to be like clockwork. He always went through the park right to the south end too, where there was a tiny strip mall with a coffee shop at one end. Morry never went into the shop but over time he'd established a waving acquaintance with the staff. Sometimes he'd wave from across the street, sometimes from in front of the window. Sometimes he knew they failed to notice him but that was good, too, for he knew that in their minds, the guy with the little dog walked past at about the same time every single night.

Morry peered through the trees and checked for traffic both ways. Nothing! Excellent! He tugged at the leash and Sooki began to move with him gratefully. She was quite used to this pause in the trees, but it was a cool night and she was keen to get home.

The Greens, Morry and Naomi, owned the first unit on the right, inside the gate of Amber Pines Retirement Community. The units were small but free-standing, each separated by rows of spruce trees, something that Morry could never figure out. Why would a place called Amber Pines plant spruce? No matter. They were good cover. Now that it was early December and thoroughly dark by evening, the trees were even more insurance against being seen. The only risk was that nosy witch, Jablonski, across the street. But — another piece in place — she'd left for her daughter's in Arizona on Monday.

7:28! Morry checked his watch before opening the front door of his little house. He'd lost a minute somehow! Must have been daydreaming. Not serious. Twelve minutes was a minimum. Odds were good he'd have more if Wes and the supervisor behaved true to form. Wes was *supposed* to stay in the guard hut until 7:30, when the supervisor was *supposed* to relieve him for his fifteen-minute break. But ever since early September, when Cherry Grind had begun working the Wednesday evening shift at the lunch counter in the rec hall, the guarding of the gate had suffered a serious decline on this mid-week day. Instead of relieving Wes at the appointed time, the supervisor had taken to waiting at the lunch counter, where he basked in the glow of Cherry's charms until Wes got there. Cherry, for her part, having only recently yielded to the reality of her age, had retired from a career as an exotic dancer and thoroughly enjoyed the attention, so that over the weeks the overlap between Wes's early arrival and the supervisor's reluctant departure had lengthened considerably.

Morry checked his coat pocket for the masking tape, and then took out his key. "Now or never," he said under his breath. Twice he tapped shakily around the keyhole before pushing in the key.

"Don't make noise!" he told himself.

But it didn't matter. Naomi was in exactly the same position as when he'd left. In fact it was the one piece of the plan he knew was a guarantee. She'd begun passing out earlier and earlier in the day over the past little while. Morry believed it was the switch to gin. Seems she couldn't put it back like the bourbon. Either way, there she was, sprawled on the couch, snoring softly, with the television set blaring. Yet, with almost magical co-ordination, there was a drink in her hand, unspilled.

The next three steps went precisely according to plan. Naomi didn't even struggle when Morry pressed the couch cushion down on her face and held it there. He was almost disappointed at that, but it meant he picked up thirty seconds. Trashing the room as kids or maybe a spaced-out druggie might do it was quick, but he'd mentally rehearsed that so often it was automatic. The final move was smooth, too. He slipped out to the back porch and carefully placed two strips of masking tape on the den window in the shape of an X. Smashing the window in was harder than he thought it would be. Good thing he used a bath towel over his elbow or he might have ripped his coat. He made a hole just large enough for an arm to be able to reach up to turn the window latch. Then he opened the window just a bit, turned, and walked down the porch steps and along to the corner of the house.

Now, back to the park. Good heavens! He'd almost forgotten the darn dog! Quickly, Morry went back in the house, grabbed Sooki, and retraced his steps. Out the back door and along the wall. Then on to the street, keeping close to the spruce trees. Good. No sign of Wes or the supervisor. That Cherry was a gift! He checked the main road for traffic and then, with Sooki protesting ever so mildly, darted across and dove into the park.

He looked at his watch. The numbers glowed 7:38. Just fine. He looked around. Nobody in the park. Too late, and it was beginning to turn cold. That was not an essential piece, but it helped. No point in trying to get to the coffee shop. Too far. Besides, the staff would think he'd passed by anyway. No, he'd wait now until 8:00, make sure Wes had returned, and then walk back through the gate and chat a minute or two with him on the way home.

 Morry Green has put all the pieces in place for a perfect murder. Except one. What one mistake has he made?

FILE #**25**

The Kid's Idea

BRENHAM STUDIOS
PRODUCTION OFFICE

Harry,

This is what the kid Mallory Hart came up with. It's pretty good — I kind of like it. Lets the audience know right up front what the Countess is like. Lot cheaper too than the big party scene Tilzer's got planned for that. See what you think. We'll have to talk it over with Tilzer but I say we shoot it no matter what he wants. Especially since the Venice set is still up — I checked this morning. Shooting won't take more than a couple hours.

Think budget!
KT

One thing: the kid thinks the scene should run BEHIND the opening credits. I think it runs on its own, right after the "Venice Italy, 1502" opener. We can do credits at the end. ???

To: Korman Telfer
From: Mallory Hart

NEW OPENING SCENE, AS YOU REQUESTED

After an establishing shot of the Doge's palace from across the canal, the camera makes a slow zoom to the balcony above right of the front portico. (This is the same balcony where the Contessa meets the French ambassador in Scene 12.) Double doors are open. Camera continues in and picks up a cardinal standing on one side of a small table. Moves closer and shows the Contessa standing on the other side. She is gowned and fully made up although it is no later than midday. The cardinal is gussied up, too, but business-like rather than churchy. Black cassock, **not** red. Red piping on it though, red sash, and the little red zuchetto on his head. Important he should look like someone who enjoys power more than holiness so that when she kills him there is probably some dark reason for it.

No dialogue in the scene that we can hear, but it's apparent the two have been talking, probably arguing. The camera has come in on a sort of intermission

There is a silver decanter on the table, two silver goblets, a flat-bladed knife, also silver — not a weapon — and a reed basket full of apples. The Contessa pours wine into each of the two goblets, pushes one toward the cardinal, picks up the other, and takes a swallow. He doesn't touch his and gives her a "do-you-think-I'm-nuts?" look, so she sets hers down, pushes it toward him, and then takes his and drinks from it. He's impressed but still wary.

She's pouty now. Offended. Offers the cardinal an apple. He smiles. Doesn't take it, and then uses both hands to remove the top layer of apples from the basket. He picks an apple from the bottom of the basket and offers it to her.

This time it's the <u>Contessa</u> who smiles. She accepts the apple and moves to take a bite but then suddenly stops and nods respectfully, almost a bow. Like she's forgotten her manners. Sets the apple on the table, spins it gently a couple of times like a top, and then cuts it in half with the knife.

The Contessa picks up one half of the apple and takes a bite, looking at the cardinal. Without taking his eyes off her, he picks up the other half and bites into it, once, then twice, before a look of realization comes over his face, followed by a flash of anger before he falls. A couple of spasms and he's dead. She's still got her half of the apple in her hand and has another bite before taking a step or two to peer down at the now still body of the cardinal.

Stays in this position until fadeout. There is a slight, bemused smile on her face. Outside sounds begin to come from the canal. They hold through the fade into Scene 1, where the gondolas approach the palace.

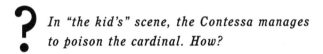

In "the kid's" scene, the Contessa manages to poison the cardinal. How?

FILE #26

The Case of the Skull & Anchor

"The two young uns 'at pulled up the skull outa Pincher Creek, they were playin' hooky." "Horse" Kahane paused to make a large contribution into the spittoon beside his desk. "'At's how come this here fishin' line's all dry now. And the bit a' rust on the plough point here. They waited, the two of 'em, coupla days afore they brought it in." He leaned out of his swivel chair, testing the outer bounds of gravity, to spit again. "They knew they were in trouble, goin' fishin' 'stead a' goin' to school. 'Course the skull scared 'em. Even a kid could tell this here's a human skull. No way they're gonna sit on a secret like that fer long."

On the other side of the battered, gray metal desk, Louis Raines-Prideau sat as far away from Horse Kahane as he could get without looking ridiculous. It didn't work. Louis Raines-Prideau, B.Sc., M.Sc., Ph.D., Fellow of the Royal Society of Forensic Anthropologists, could not have looked more out of place in the office of Deputy Sheriff Jimmy Don Kahane if he had been a Wedgwood tea service. Yet this was not the first time he'd been here. Over the seven years Louis Raines-Prideau had been chair of the department of anthropology at the state university, the deputy had invoked an agreement between the state and the school on two previous occasions to use Louis's forensic skills.

On the desk, in addition to Horse Kahane's booted feet, lay a human skull, a cranium actually: a skull without a lower jaw. A piece of nylon fishing line encircled it at the cheekbones. The line was knotted at the back of the skull, and led to a heavy triangular piece of iron, sharply pointed at the apex. This was the plough point Horse had referred to. Whoever had tossed the skull into Pincher Creek had used the piece of metal as an anchor.

"Do you have any objection to my cutting the fishing line free?" Louis Raines-Prideau wanted to get on with things.

"Anythin' yuh want, Louis." Horse pronounced the name 'Loo-ee,' in two distinct syllables. "The kids been handlin' it so there's no prints. 'Sides, it's been in the water."

Louis Raines-Prideau took a thin leather case from the inside pocket of his suit coat and extracted a long, narrow pair of scissors. Working quickly, for he suspected the deputy was due to use the spittoon again, he carefully wedged one blade of the scissors between the skull and the line and made the cut.

"Yuh see, what I think I'm gonna have to do . . ." Horse Kahane tried to lean over the spittoon again but found that somehow he'd gotten overextended, so he pulled his feet off the desk to get closer. He spit. ". . . Like I say, what I gotta do, I think, is drag that creek. See, the way I figure, the rest a' the body's in there. In parts, like this here skull. But yuh see, what I need to know . . . I mean . . . any chance yuh kin tell me maybe how long the thing's been in there? In the creek. Stuff like that. The way I figure, whoever did the shooting, cut 'im up. Or her. Then spread the parts in the creek. Doesn't take long fer crayfish to eat the meat off like they did on the skull here."

Louis found himself inching closer to the sheriff's desk — and the forbidding spittoon. He couldn't suppress the challenge of forensic analysis.

"You're right about 'shot,'" he said. "That's a bullet hole here in the upper cranial vault. But it's an exit hole. Where the bullet went out." In spite of himself he leaned close to Horse. "See how it's beveled? Narrow on the inside, then wider outside? That means the bullet came out this way. No other holes, so perhaps it entered through the mouth or the lower jaw."

Horse Kahane's childlike expression showed genuine fascination.

"But in my opinion," Louis went on, "there are no more body parts in the creek. I'll grant you, whoever threw this in there was certainly trying to get rid of it. But this cran—, er, skull, has been sitting around for some time, maybe on a shelf or in a drawer. The crayfish didn't eat the . . . er . . . er . . . *meat* because there was none on it when it went into the creek."

"None on it?" Kahane absently stuck his left inside finger into his mouth and excavated a large, soggy wad of tobacco. "How'd you figure that?"

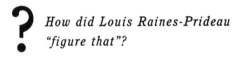 *How did Louis Raines-Prideau "figure that"?*

FILE # 27

Milverton's Deception

*A single dimmed spotlight picks up **Milverton** seated at a small but very ornately carved wooden desk at center stage. He is facing the audience but is turned slightly toward stage right. **Milverton** is dressed in the formal morning suit of a mid- to late-nineteenth-century butler. On the desk are two fairly substantial leather-bound books and an inkwell from which protrudes a thin metal stylus. On one corner of the desk is a small kerosene lamp; it is not lit, although in front of it burn two candles, each in a quite ordinary and func-tional candleholder. **Milverton**'s white hair gleams in the light, but his face is not easily made out. Even harder to see are the features of the man who stands facing him on the other side of the desk. He is young, and appears to be, like **Milverton**, in service.*

Milverton   I have recommended to Lady Tottenham that you not be dismissed from her service, at least for the time being . . .

Birdwell   Oh, thank you, sir!

Milverton   . . . but the outcome will depend entirely on your ability to manage the matter of these two books.

Birdwell   Yes, sir.

Milverton It's an opportunity to redeem yourself, Birdwell. After all, it was you who shelved them improperly here in the library.

Birdwell Yes, sir, but —

Milverton You know, Birdwell, in fact, everyone in service here knows, that her ladyship requires certain proprieties be observed. And one of these, Birdwell, is that in her library, the works of . . . er . . . *female* authors are to be shelved separately. It is not proper, in her ladyship's opinion — and quite so — that these should stand pressed against books written by men.

Birdwell Indeed, sir, and . . .

Milverton So that when it was revealed recently that this novelist George Eliot is really that scandalous Marian Evans person, her ladyship was profoundly embarrassed. For you had two works by this Eliot, or Evans, woman, *Middlemarch* here, and — what is the other one? — yes, *Mill on the Floss*; you had them shelved with male authors, Birdwell! You're assigned responsibility for the library because you have some education, Birdwell. You are supposed to be aware of details like this. It's not as though the Evans woman has taken pains to disguise her way of living!

Birdwell I was engaged in . . .

Milverton And then — *then* — when I take steps to ensure that the proprieties are observed, what do I discover? Two weeks pass, two full weeks, before you move them to their place in proper alphabetical order with the other *female* authors.

Birdwell With respect, sir, if you recall, all this occurred at the time Lady Tottenham was expecting the visit from Her Majesty and we were constantly being summoned to extra duty. I barely had . . .

Milverton Precisely why you are being given exceptional leeway, Birdwell. Now to the matter at hand. While they sat there, with the *male* authors,

both volumes were damaged by a worm or some
burrowing creature that's eaten all the way from the
title page of *Middlemarch* clear through to the end
page of *The Mill on the Floss*. The covers will have
to be replaced, of course, but I am assured by the
printers that they can repair the individual pages,
even the hand-drawn illustrations. It will be
expensive. Twelve pounds, sixpence for those hundreds of pages, but for her ladyship's own reasons
these books are very important to her and she
wants it done.

Birdwell   Sir . . .

Milverton   Off with you then, Birdwell. Take the money
and the books to the printer and see this through.
Off with you! And remember, you are on probation.
I expect you to be grateful for this opportunity.

*The spotlight comes up slightly, just enough to reveal **Birdwell** as
he turns to the audience and lifts the books, one in each hand, in
exasperation.*

*Birdwell is exasperated because he realizes that
Milverton must be engaging in a fraudulent deal
with the printer. What is the deception?*

Fishing out of Season

"**Y**ou can't get hold of him? Tomorrow's May the fourteenth! The hearing! What do you mean you can't get hold of him?" Chief Park Warden B. Vernon Smith was shouting out his open office door at the department's beleaguered secretary.

"Just what I said! I can't get hold of him! You want me to draw pictures?" Lil Murphy was much admired by the assistant wardens for being completely unintimidated by their volatile boss.

"He's in Virgin Gorda," she continued, "and if you watched the news, like normal people, you'd know that a hurricane took out everything there yesterday."

"Virgin Gorda! That's in . . . isn't that in the Caribbean? Why there?" Warden Smith was still yelling, unaware that Lil was now standing in the doorway, a fist on one hip and some papers in her other hand.

"Maybe that's as far as he could afford to get from here!" Lil said, moving to the chief's desk and tossing the papers in front of him. "Here's his notes. There's a sheet for each time he followed them out."

"But I need a surveillance *report*! With names and dates and what type of fish were caught and . . . well . . . like that!"

The chief was glaring at her but she was utterly unmoved. "You don't have a report," she said. "You got notes."

"Notes!" Smith shuffled the few sheets of notepad paper. "This is all gobbledygook. Look at this one! Dated a week ago. Says . . . says . . . how'm I supposed to *read* this? Says Hesson . . . no . . . Hes—"

Lil took the paper out of the chief's hand. "It says 'Hester Long: trout' and 'Francis Cadeux: whitefish.'"

Chief Smith didn't reply. He was subconsciously groping about for ways to get more help from Lil without losing face. The "he" who had neglected to complete a formal report was an assistant warden assigned to an anti-poaching task force, part of a park service program to catch people who were taking fish before the various seasons opened. The missing assistant warden had been in charge of a special surveillance of four local residents who always went out together, and the upcoming hearing would determine whether he had gathered enough information to lay charges against them.

"That was the day before he went on vacation, so it would be the last time he went out," the chief said, stating the obvious.

Lil pressed her lips together tightly.

"Let's see," Smith shuffled the papers again, then selected one of the sheets. "This one, now," he said. "Here's your Hester Long again."

"She's not *my* Hester Long."

"Says she took whitefish this time out. What's the date? April 29. That's opening day for whitefish. Trout, too. Hmm . . . no violation there. And who's this one? Gabriel Long. Husband or brother? No matter, he took bass. That's OK, too, 'cause bass season starts April 23." He turned the sheet over twice, and then held it to the light briefly. "Doesn't say anything else."

"Never was much of a writer," Lil said.

"Now here." Chief Warden Smith picked up a third sheet. "Now here!" He waved the sheet at Lil Murphy. "This is why I want formal *reports*! Here you got the Longs again, a week before her whitefish trip. And Cadeux. And this fourth name. What's it say?"

"Fabian March," Lil answered without looking at the paper. "That was the first time he followed them out." She leaned over the desk until her face was very close to Smith's. "We've had our eye on the four of them for some time, you know."

"We have? Yes, of course we have." He waved the paper again, this time less vigorously. "But this doesn't say anything. Just says 'each one caught' and then there's these four different . . . well . . . *squiggles*!"

"Code," Lil explained, again without looking.

"Yeah, but what does it mean? And why use code anyway?"

Lil shrugged. "I just work here."

Smith held the paper for a few seconds and then set it down in favor of the fourth and last sheet. "May 3," he read. "'Francis Cadeux: trout'; 'Fabian March' — I can read it this time — 'Fabian March: pike.' No problem on pike. Season's been open two months now. But these people, they . . . it's funny . . . It seems that each time they went out, no two of them took the same species."

"And not only that."

"What?"

"None of them ever took the same species twice."

"Where does it say that?"

"It doesn't, but that's what he told me when he gave me the notes."

Chief Warden Smith raised his head slowly. There was a suggestion of a smile on his lips. "You know, I think I'm going to be ready for the hearing after all. There's at least three fish-and-game law violations on that first trip out!" He gathered up the sheets. "Sometimes, Murphy . . . sometimes you are most helpful!"

Lil raised her chin slightly.

"I just work here," she said.

 What is the date of the first trip out? And what are the three fish-and-game law violations on this first trip? Who committed them?

The Last Wish
of Latimer Orkin

An odor of formaldehyde permeated the room like some deep-rooted sin for which there was neither penance nor forgiveness. It clung to the furniture, soaked through the worn gray linoleum, and hung on the faded drapes. Nona knew her clothes would smell of it, too, by the time she left. People would stare at her on the subway and give her a wide berth, as though to touch her would mean acknowledging something desperate and final. It's not so bad, she wanted to say to them, not as bad as the stink the senior partners raise with their vile cigars! And when you're a lowly law student, you have to put up with it, along with doing all the Joe jobs, like picking up autopsy reports and forensic data.

In her not-yet-launched legal career, this was already Nona's third visit to the city's forensics lab, and she had still to decide which was worse: the smell of formaldehyde or the stale smoke that blanketed all three floors at Makavel and Quislin. At least here, she thought, as she shifted on the hard metal chair, there was a break from time to time, if only because old Doctor Tranh got up every fifteen minutes to go to the bathroom. He'd left again just seconds ago, and she knew from experience that at least five minutes would pass before he came back.

Nona used the opportunity to read once again the hastily scribbled last will of Latimer Orkin. The handwriting was barely legible, but there was no doubt about what the words said.

I leave all my worldly goods to my friend Misty Duvall.

Underneath it, somewhat more carefully written, was the signature of Latimer Orkin, and, more important, beneath that was the date. That date was also the day of his death. Still lower down was the beginning of a sentence that appeared to be the words *I am of soun*— but a thin, unsteady line fell away from the "n," offering strong evidence that death or unconsciousness had come at that moment.

Orkin had been found in his bedroom, lying face down on the floor. The night table had been knocked over, its single drawer pulled right out of the slides. A lamp was smashed and the telephone knocked off its cradle, but Orkin appeared to have achieved his last objective. With an expensive mechanical pencil found in his hand, he had written, or was believed — certainly by Misty Duvall, although most emphatically not by his three children — to have written a new but final will on a small spiral notepad.

Naturally, the circumstances of his death had attracted the police. And the circumstances of the will had, in turn, involved various legal firms. Makavel and Quislin had been retained by Orkin's children.

The sound of flushing echoed down the tiled corridor and Nona sat back to wait for Doctor Tranh.

"And there was very large liver." Usually, after these frequent sojourns, the doctor announced his return by finishing whatever thought or sentence was in the air when he left. "Must have been drinker. But cause of death coronary infarction. Heart attack. Not foul play."

Nona leaned forward. "That will be your report?"

"Not written yet. More work to do."

"You mean you're going to do the handwriting analysis, too?"

"Handwriting analysis no use. This writing too messy. Not everyday style for this man. I mean other work. You want to see?"

"Sure!" Nona knew the old man was kind of sweet on her. Most of the other law students who came to the lab were male first timers who always made the subconsciously racist assumption that Tranh was the janitor. She watched him take Orkin's mechanical pencil out of a plastic evidence bag. It looked pricey. The casing was pewter with thin inlaid strips of mother-of-pearl.

"First time out of bag," Doctor Tranh said. "In old days this called an 'Eversharp.' Come, we look for fingerprints."

At first, Nona's intent was to humor the old man, but, as he explained the principle of vacuum-metal deposition for visualizing fingerprints on smooth surfaces, she became completely drawn in. It took but a brief time to confirm that the only prints on the pen were definitely Orkin's.

"Now we use S.E.M. Scanning electron microscope. Very fancy. Come sit here before monitor." The old man was definitely enjoying himself. He handed Nona a rubber glove, along with the pencil and a blank page from the notebook containing the will.

"You write something now," he said, twisting the lead up out of the pencil. "Pretend it your will! Glove protect fingerprints."

Warily, Nona took up the task. She wrote Orkin's words but frowned when she realized immediately that her effort was far more legible.

Doctor Tranh didn't notice. He was far more excited by the two images on the computer screen. "See! This original writing by dead man. This yours. Mark on paper exactly the same, so this definitely the pencil used."

Nona felt herself being drawn further in and could sense Doctor Tranh picking up on her interest. It occurred to her that his next trip to the facility was long overdue.

"Now best instrument of all!" he crowed. "Gas chromatograph and mass spectrometer." For the first time, his accent buried completely any sense of what he was saying, but Nona soon understood what he was about. The equipment enabled her to see that the bits of fluff stuck to the spiraling wire of the notebook were of precisely the same composition as bits taken from the drawer.

"That means almost for sure the notebook must have come from the drawer of his night table," she said.

"Indeed!"

"And the fingerprints are all his."

"Ah!"

"And this is definitely the pencil used to write the will."

"There is no doubt."

"So, on the surface, the available evidence shows that as he was dying Latimer Orkin really did write a last will leaving everything to Misty Duvall."

"Very much so."

"But whoever actually wrote this so-called will made one big mistake."

"You are very clever young lady!"

 What mistake was made by "whoever actually wrote this so-called will"?

FILE # 30

Death in
Benton County

Polly Dersam leaned against the trunk of the unmarked cruiser, lifted her face to the bright spring sun, and then drew up one leg to hook a heel on top of the bumper. There would be warm comfort like this for only a few more minutes before the sun dropped behind the hills rimming the horizon. Polly lifted her chin higher and closed her eyes. She wasn't avoiding the death site in front of her. It wasn't going anywhere in any case. What she was doing was letting go just for a bit, enjoying the reassurance that, after a particularly cruel winter, summer indeed was going to return as it always had.

Later, while driving back to the station, Polly admitted to herself that she may have been a bit too relaxed, for Jackson Grit was right beside her before she even realized he was there. Not good police practice on her part, especially now, with the whole county abuzz over the possibility of a serial killer.

"Wher' was yuh yestiddy?" None of the Grits made small talk and Jackson, as head of the clan, set the example. "If yuh'd a been here, mighta been diffrint fer them other cops. Th' boy, he was some scared."

"The boy" was Jackson Grit's twenty-year-old son, Jerome,

youngest of the four males in this backwoods, rough-and-tumble family. He was deaf and mute, and although most of the infamous Grits enjoyed the privilege of a name, Jerome was "The Grit Boy" throughout Benton County, and to his family, just "Th' boy." Yesterday afternoon, it had taken pepper spray and six Benton deputies to get Jerome into a cruiser and put him in a cell at the county jail. Two of the six deputies were on hospital leave today.

"He know'd he done wrong takin' down that Injun like that. But he's some slow, th' boy, yuh know that better'n most. An' he don't talk, he don't hear. When he seen all them cops comin' at 'im . . . well . . . An' his brothers, whaddaya 'spect them tuh do? All them cops. See . . . yuh'd a been here, mighta helped. Boy knows yuh. Knows yuh unnerstan 'im."

Over several years of dealing with the legendary Grits in a ceaseless string of assaults, drunk and disorderlies, property damages, and an occasional extortion, Polly Dersam had earned the family's grudging respect. Her cause was helped by the fact that she seemed to have a kind of empathy with Jerome, and it was boosted significantly by the support of "Old Mary," the Grits' alpha female, who'd decked one of her older sons with a frying pan for making a drunken pass at Polly while she brought him home one freezing night.

"Wuz right this same time yestiddy it happen'd. Maybe a few minutes earlier. Saw it m'self from the kitchen winda plain 's day. Th' boy, he wuz pokin' a stick inta th' pool there . . ."

Polly pulled her gaze away from the absorbing topography of Jackson Grit's face to look at the pool just a few steps in front of them. It wasn't large. With the beginning of the spring runoff now, and with the ice gone, it was perhaps just a bit bigger than the car she'd backed up to the death site. The pool was fed by a small stream that crossed the back of the Grits' barnyard. She knew it was a favorite spot of Jerome's.

"Ever' spring he's down here, soon 's th' ice 's gone, lookin' fer suckers. Snares 'em he does. Good at it, too. Anyways, he's got th' stick in th' pool . . ." Jackson stopped to scratch himself with complete absorption in the task. Polly focused even harder on the pool.

"Lookin' fer suckers, like I say, an' th' Injun just *appears*! Comes outa the cedar trees here. Like I did just now. Yuh could see from th' kitchen, an' yuh knew what was gonna happen, but there's no way I could do nothin'. Th' Injun he comes up behind th' boy, and yuh know he don't hear but soon 's he sees a shadow over 'im he's up swingin' round with th' stick!"

Jackson stopped to scratch again. Polly moved a little farther away from the car.

"Just a plain accident!" Jackson was becoming agitated. "No way that boy'd do nothin' like that deliberate. But even he knows 'bout that killer Injun 'round the county now. Why Ol' Mary, she . . ."

"Jackson!" Polly spoke for the first time. "Jackson, no one knows yet who has done those killings."

"Then whattabout that Injun stuff with th' bodies?"

Benton County had become aroused by an unprecedented three murders in less than three months. Each had taken place in a rural area, and at each scene investigators had found what appeared to be ceremonial items used by the Ojibwa people, of whom there were many in the area.

"Think about it, Jackson: You've lived all your life here in the county. Ever know a native person to leave one of their sacred pieces behind?"

"But . . ."

"Doesn't matter!" Polly cut him off. "That's not why I'm here. Just came to see the scene for myself. I want you to know I'm sorry I wasn't here yesterday. Was in Toronto. Didn't get back till just before noon today. I'm sorry, and you be sure to tell Mary that, too. And tell her, just as I'm telling you, that I've already been to see Jerome. When I go off duty as soon as I get back, I'll go see him again."

That assurance seemed to have an effect on Jackson Grit.

"Yuh sure yuh won't have tea or nothin'? Ol' Mary allus likes to see yuh."

Polly moved back to her car and got in. "I have to go, Jackson," she said, rolling down the window, "but I'll be back tomorrow."

She drove off slowly, but even before her cruiser passed the litter of rusted implements that bracketed both sides of the laneway, a feeling of depression hit her, for Polly knew that tomorrow's visit would be a tough one. Ferreting out the truth is never easy in the first place, especially in cases of violent death. Because the Grits were involved, that job would be even harder this time.

 Polly Dersam has apparently picked up a flaw in Jackson Grit's account of the events of yesterday. What is that flaw?

FILE # 31

The Coroner's Decision

OFFICE OF DANA STEELE, CHIEF CORONER, TAMWORTH COUNTY

Case #184-00:   Avia Lund-March, deceased

Summary of Inquest and Findings

Date of Inquest: 17 January 2001
Purpose of Inquest: To determine cause of death
Chair: D. Steele, M.D., F.R.S.C., A.F.P., N.E.H.H.

Witnesses: Luigi de Carma (superintendent of Hampshire Towers), Staff Sgt. Brenda Donnelly (investigating officer), Reginald March (spouse of deceased), Dr. S.D. Sharma (pathologist).

Statement of Fact: At or about 11:20 a.m., on the morning of 9 August 2000, subject Avia Lund-March died of injuries sustained in a fall from the balcony of her apartment on the twelfth floor of Hampshire Towers, at 200 Hampshire Blvd., in the city of Seneca.

Testimony: Staff Sgt. Brenda Donnelly testifies that she was summoned to 200 Hampshire Blvd. on the date in question in response to a 9-1-1 call made by Luigi de Carma (see witness list above). At the scene she found a 42-year-old Caucasian female on the sidewalk that fronts the building. Subject appeared to have extensive injuries and exhibited no vital signs. (Latter fact confirmed in ambulance report; see appendix.) Sgt. Donnelly further testifies that after securing the scene she located only two witnesses, L. de Carma and R. March (see below for testimony).

Body of deceased lay face up, at a point 16 1/2 feet from the front (south) wall of the building at 200 Hampshire Blvd. Photographs supplied by Sgt. Donnelly are in the attached evidence file.

Pathologist Dr. Sharma testifies that subject likely died instantly of massive neural trauma. An autopsy was unable to identify any injuries that would not have resulted from the fall. There was no evidence of alcohol or narcotics or medication in body of deceased. Dr. Sharma produced medical records showing deceased was in good health leading up to this incident. Subject deceased was 5 feet, 3 inches tall and weighed 118 pounds.

Building superintendent L. de Carma testifies that he was repairing a light fixture in front of 200 Hampshire Blvd. at the time of the incident and saw the final seconds of subject's fall and the contact with the sidewalk. Witness testifies that the event was traumatic for him, and he is currently receiving medical attention as a result. Mr. de Carma states that the deceased and her husband lease unit 1246 on the twelfth floor of Hampshire Towers. There are fourteen units per floor in this building, and the four corner units on each floor have double balconies. Unit 1246 is one such unit and has a balcony facing south and one facing east. The balconies project 3 feet from the exterior wall, and have wrought iron railings 5 feet high.

L. de Carma asserts that the balcony railings are well maintained and in excellent repair.

When questioned by the chair, Mr. de Carma replies that he knew of no difficulty between subject deceased and her husband, that they had occupied Unit 1246 for three years, and that from his perspective, they were model tenants.

Reginald March is husband of the subject deceased. He testifies that they had been married for nineteen years and that the marriage was generally without difficulties.

On the morning of the incident, Mr. March states, he was drinking coffee with subject deceased in the room that opens to the south-facing balcony. According to the witness, subject deceased was a "flower-fanatic," and was distressed to see that the clematis vines she had planted in boxes on the balcony were not trailing properly along the wires she had installed for that purpose. Thus, Mr. March testifies, she went onto the balcony and stood on a chair to reach up to the wires. When she put one foot on the edge of the railing he called to her to wait and went to a storage closet in the kitchen to get a stepladder. According to Mr. March, he believed the subject deceased to have fallen from the balcony while he was on his way to the kitchen because he heard a short scream or yell just as he got to the closet.*

*Note from Chief Coroner Steele: At this point in his account, Mr. March broke down, and it appeared he would be unable to continue. However, in the opinion of the chair, there is now sufficient evidence on which to make a ruling. Therefore I have adjourned the hearing **sine die**, and rule as follows:

 Chief Coroner Steele has three options: accidental death, suicide, homicide. Which should he choose, and why?

FILE # **32**

Where to
Send the Dogs

The heavy dark clouds behind him in the southwest were yet another reason for the tension Michael de Sousa was feeling. At both ends of the valley, the engineers were doing everything they could to control the flow of water over the dams, but time was now precious. As soon as the three kids had been reported missing, before Michael had even made the calls that would set up the search, the first thing he'd done was get the Humber Conservation Authority to close down the Step One dam and increase the flow over Step Two.

It was not an easy thing. Because of the heavy rainfall over the past several days, a high level of water was pouring over the dams. Altering the flow was dangerous, especially at Step One. It was the oldest of the three dams in the valley, and the only one built on earth banks. Not that the engineers didn't care about the missing kids; they were as concerned as anyone. But what they didn't want was to take responsibility for what could be a greater disaster. If Step One broke, a flash flood would barrel down to Middle Lake, where Michael was standing now, and raise it to a point where Step Two might not hold.

It was a newer dam, Step Two, made of concrete. But it had a reputation for problems. No one, not the engineers, not the Authority, and certainly not the villagers living between it and the brand new Step Three dam, had any faith in it. Therefore, as it turned out, the responsibility became Michael's. Rather than use up time arguing with the engineers, he had used his emergency powers as head of Search and Rescue and ordered Step One closed.

That was four hours ago. For Michael, it had been four hours of chaos: calling in sector heads to lead the search teams; organizing the teams into grids; sending vitally important office staff out to every saloon in the county to find Jimmy McConachie, whose bloodhounds would be needed; squabbling with the police over who was actually in charge; and, on top of it all, coping with three sets of hysterical parents. It had taken this long, too, before Michael could get down into the valley himself, and another twenty minutes before he could extract himself from the mobile command center to reconnoiter along the now receding shores of Middle Lake. His long stride had soon taken him well down the hiking trail where the kids had told their parents they were going.

At a point where the trail forked, one path veering left by the lake, and another leading sharply right toward a thick, barely penetrable growth of mature rhododendron, Michael slowed for a moment and knelt to catch his breath. The nervousness was making him tired and edgy. He would much rather have been leading a sector team. At least there was action.

He got up and moved down the lake path, then knelt again, absently pushing his fingers into a ridgeline of dead pine needles and maple keys that ran along the middle of it. What he was doing, for the third time in the past five minutes, was straining to hear the sound of water boiling over Step One and hoping that he wouldn't. Yet, at the same time he was reassured by the silence, it disturbed him, too. Even though it was late fall — almost winter — there should have been the noise of birds. Blue jays, at least. Maybe a cardinal and, certainly, chickadees.

Michael stood and looked over his shoulder yet again at the

lowering sky. More heavy rain coming, no question. How bad? he wondered. Was that why there were no birds? A big rain would mean Step One had to be opened again. There would be no choice. Time, time. They had to find those kids and soon.

A noise pushed into his consciousness, vague at first but soon sharply defined, as one of the sector teams approached with Jimmy McConachie and his dogs. They weren't barking. Another silence to bother Michael. Contrary to the Hollywood way of portraying things, bloodhounds rarely bark unless they are excited, and they usually don't get excited until their quarry's scent is really strong.

Michael met the team at the fork and pointed to the rhododendrons. When Jimmy drew back his head and squinted dubiously with one eye, Michael pointed more emphatically.

"The kids were on this side of the lake. That much we know," he said. "You've got an hour, Jimmy. Maybe a couple. And you can't cover the two trails in that time. If the kids are still in the valley, and if your dogs find their scent, it'll be that way."

 Why is Michael de Sousa so sure the kids went that way and not along the fork to the left?

FILE # 33

Time for the Mortars?

Although the ridge was over a mile away, the entire battalion could see the lone rider galloping hell-for-leather toward them, for a column of red Crimean dust hung in the still air all along his route. On the valley floor, where the river looped to the east, two Russian officers were watching the rider with great interest. They stood out from the group behind them because, having conceded to the unusual heat, both had removed their shakos, and the sun was lighting up their white-blond hair. However, their tunics were buttoned to the top even though the high collars were fringed with ermine. The senior officer, a colonel, was holding his shako under one arm. Not the other, a major; he was watching the rider with a long telescope that required both hands to hold.

"It's the Thracian," the latter finally said in a confirming tone.

The colonel nodded once and without turning around, raised his free hand and snapped his fingers. "Translator!" he commanded, in a voice that was surprisingly youthful. He was indeed young. Colonel Sergei Sergeivich Mikhail Gregor Korovsky was only twenty-two. He was also a count, and his father was a key player in Tsar Nicholas's inner circle.

"Yes, Excellency!" A non-commissioned officer at the edge of the group detached himself and began to run past a long row of mortars toward the supply wagons.

The colonel turned to a heavily whiskered captain, considerably older than himself. "Bring the reserve mortars forward. I want a semi-circle opening northwest."

"Excellency." The captain brought his hand to the visor of his shako in a manner that would have been punished on the parade ground and walked away in the same direction as the non-com.

The major lifted the telescope to his eye again, then put it down. His name was Fyodor and he was only sixteen. He was Sergei's brother.

"The Thracian's seen something; that's for sure." Fyodor's cheeks were flushed with excitement. "Sergei, if there are troops on the other side of the ridge, and if they're French, will you fire on them?" he asked.

A cavalry unit had delivered orders that morning, instructing Sergei to hold back his battalion to protect the flank of Russian forces retreating from Balaklava. Although the Imperial army had inflicted very heavy losses on the base there over the past several weeks, it had been unable to dislodge the British and their French allies. Normally, the Russians would have expected to withdraw without too much interference, but a bizarre, suicidal charge yesterday by a British light cavalry brigade — across an open field, directly at a battery of heavy guns! — had made the Imperial command wary. Sergei had scouts out in every direction.

Fyodor repeated, quietly so the others couldn't hear, "Will you put mortar fire over the ridge? If they're French?" The two brothers, like so many Russians, had a very soft spot for anything French. "Or, God forbid, what if they're our troops? What are you going to do? You know we can't afford to . . ."

The black look on his brother's face stopped him. Sergei and Fyodor would much rather have been riding with a cavalry brigade, the honor and glamor troops of the Russian Imperial army — or of any other European army for that matter — but at

Balaklava they had been demoted to an artillery unit for failing to take down a company of French, caught in the open and defenseless.

Sergei spoke slowly and deliberately through clenched teeth. "If I have to, I will bring the fires of hell down on . . ."

The rest of his sentence was drowned out in a shuffle of hoof beats and shouts and other noise as the scout clattered up to the officers. "The Thracian" — he had no other name, at least not one that anyone used — knew the area well. He'd been with the battalion for several weeks now. But young as the two officers were, they had no illusions about the man's loyalty. His type went with the highest bidder. But like all officers in the Imperial Command, they counted on the Thracian's hatred of the Turks. Since the Russians were attacking Turkey, it made sense to use him.

He was already babbling away in a glot of Bulgarian and Turkish and Greek that only one man in the battalion could understand.

"He says it's infantry, Excellency," the translator reported, as Sergei approached. "French. At least a battalion from the sound of it."

Another flurry of unintelligible speech.

"And they are less than an hour behind our supply wagons."

"That means, Excellency," it was one of the other officers, an older one, "that we must begin a barrage right away!"

Sergei held up his hand palm out in a halt sign. "Ask the Thracian . . ." he stopped suddenly, realizing he still carried his shako under his arm. He put it on, adding to his height and to what he knew would be regal bearing. "Ask him how he knows they're French."

A rapid exchange.

"Their flag, Excellency."

Fyodor stepped closer and spoke softly to Sergei with his back to the others. "Does he know the French flag from ours?"

"Good point." Sergei turned to the translator. "Ask him to describe the flag."

"Forgive me, Excellency. He's already said it was three stripes. Red, white, and blue."

"Then ask him if the stripes were horizontal or vertical."

Another short burst.

"Excellency, he says vertical."

Fyodor could barely contain his excitement. "Shall I prepare for fire?"

Sergei lifted both hands and removed his shako again. He started to speak and then, in deference to his brother, led him away from the group. "Fyodor. Do you want us to be in the artillery forever? Or, worse, in the infantry? No, we will not fire. The Thracian is concocting something, so you will now take your telescope and get up to that ridge to see what's on the other side."

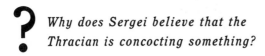

Why does Sergei believe that the
Thracian is concocting something?

FILE # 34

When Bad Things Come in Threes

Until the third incident at the Happy Sunbeam Nursery School, no one paid much attention. They didn't even call the police for the first two. On Monday a shutter had come loose from one of the second-floor windows and crashed to the playground below. A new shutter, too. Fortunately, all the children had just left the area for snack time, and, except for the fact that the shutter was beyond repair, there was no damage. Then, on Tuesday, a loose brick from one of the several unused chimneys on the north wall had come down in a strong wind. This time there was damage. The parents' drop-off drive was on the north side and the brick had landed on the roof of a car.

Perhaps it was the secret pleasure the staff felt over the brick's choice of car that diverted any thoughts that there might be sabotage afoot. The gray Volvo sedan was driven by one of the more vocal mothers, who continually tested the two-minute stopping limit in the drop-off drive while she went into the school to assert her opinions. But the third incident, only a week later — that gave one pause.

The Kindergym in the playground collapsed. Only one of the dozen or so three-year-olds crawling on it was hurt. Not seriously.

A broken arm. Technically just a greenstick fracture, so that, once his initial tears dried and the shock wore off, his celebrity status, significantly enhanced by a wide bandage and a bright blue sling, more than made up for the brief pain. Unfortunately for Moira Nairn, principal of Happy Sunbeam, and her staff, the injured boy's mother wrote for a local tabloid. Her subsequent piece, "Bad Things Come in Threes?" hit a slow news day and ran on the front page of the morning edition.

It made for a long day for Moira. By late afternoon, according to her secretary's calculations, fully three-quarters of the parents had called, wanting to know more about the "sabotage" the article hinted at. Now, at dusk, Moira found herself out behind the school, probing gingerly through the remains of the Kindergym. The janitors had piled the pieces in a fenced-off portion of the yard where the school kept other discarded equipment that yielded to the amazing power of three-year-olds to destroy. The fallen shutter and the brick were back here, too, and, with the Kindergym, were isolated in a pile of disgrace in one corner of the yard.

Moira picked up one of the failed support braces from the gym and turned it over in her hands. Clearly, it had broken the way one would expect a piece of wood to break, split along the grain. No evidence of a saw cut or of prying by a chisel. "Nothing wrong with this," she said aloud. The same was true of several other pieces. For some reason, the wood from the gym seemed far more intact than the wood from the shutter.

"Smithereens," Moira spoke aloud again, as she picked up a shattered piece of the latter. But then, the shutter had had farther to fall, and the wood was lighter, too. Moira turned her attention back to the Kindergym and tried to pick up a piece of chain, but both ends of it were still attached to heavy sections and she couldn't budge it. Another hunk of chain yielded easily at first, but, as she looked closer in the fading light, she could see that the other end was still securely fastened, as it was supposed to be.

"That bolt." Talking out loud to herself was not just a habit. It always seemed to help her thought process. "It's from the Kindergym." The bolt was about the length of her middle finger but thicker than her thumb. She ran her fingers along the length of the thread. "Nothing wrong with this either, looks like." Moira held it closer. The manufacturer's name was stamped on the head, but, with the light coating of rust, and in the gathering darkness, she couldn't read it.

When she tossed it back into the pile, it fell into a gap and then made a clink, an odd noise that drew her attention. The noise . . . it was worth investigating, but she didn't really want to reach into the pile. One of the well-kept secrets of the school was that rats had been seen back here. Still, the sound was just too interesting. She put her hands on her knees and bent over, then finally squatted down and reached somewhat timidly into the gap where the bolt had disappeared. There was something . . . it felt funny.

"Of course! The brick! The offending brick!" With more confidence, she grabbed the guilty piece of masonry and pulled it out. One corner was broken off. Mortar still clung to it. The brick, too, had a manufacturer's stamp. The name was imprinted on one of the wide surfaces in quite large letters, but when Moira found she could not read it, she realized it was far too dark now to turn up anything useful. Still, she decided to take the brick into her office and have a close look at it. "Who knows?" she said, at the same time admitting to herself, silently, that she really wasn't very sure if she — or anyone, for that matter — could identify sabotage on a brick unless it was dramatically obvious.

One thing did catch her eye, however. As she walked around to the front of the school and into the strong lighting in the yard, she could read the name on the brick. McNab. That amused her. It was one letter off from the name of the tabloid reporter, who was MacNab.

"If nothing else — yuck!" she said, as she noticed that her little excursion had brought on a dry cleaning bill. The cuffs of her pants were smudged with grime.

"That's grease on my knee, too, darn it! And what's that?"

There was a reddish-brown streak just below her waist. "From the brick?" She continued muttering as she opened the front door of the school and waited for the security system to set itself. Then it dawned on her.

"Flashlight! Gotta get a flashlight and get back out there. No. Maybe I should leave it there and call the police. Yes, that's a better idea. Get 'em here now without kids or parents around. See if they agree with me that there has been some tampering in at least one of these incidents."

 What did Moira Nairn discover during her visit to the backyard that now leads her to believe there may have been "some tampering" in at least one of the three incidents at Happy Sunbeam Nursery School?

FILE # 35

Incident at
Garibaldi Park

M E M O R A N D U M

TRANS-BORDER INVESTIGATIVE SERVICES, INC.

To: Edwina Gadarene, Manager: Claims & Distributions, Access Insurance Inc.

From: Morris Freeman,
Trans-Border Investigative Services, Inc.

Regarding: Claim #2740-15-XT:
Packet Freight Forwarders
Equipment Damage, 30 June 2000

Date: 15 July 2000

Enclosed is the claim form completed by Eugene Packet, as well as the incident report by Constable Gary Sheaf of the Royal Canadian Mounted Police. As we discussed on the telephone yesterday, Mr. Packet is attempting a bit of a scam in his claim. A pretty clumsy one, though. My advice would be to confront him with it and get him to re-file the claim. However, you probably wouldn't want to keep him as a client.

In my opinion, the charges against Duffy and Vaughn-Widmer will not hold up in court, if they even reach that point. Too hard to prove. On the other hand, both of them have signed statements that can't be truthful. Therefore, it should be possible to recover damages either from them or from their organizations (BFW and SOS, respectively) by means of a civil action. It's worth pursuing because they'd likely settle out of court to save embarrassment.

M. Freeman

Access Insurance Incorporated
* *

STANDARD CLAIM FORM

(Please complete this form as accurately as possible in your own words. Access Insurance advises that, when completed and signed, this form may constitute a legal document in the states of Washington and Montana, and in the province of British Columbia.)

Name of claimant: *Packet Freight Forwarders*

Policy #: *15-XT-66107*

Name of person completing this form: *Eugene Packet*

Are you the policy holder? (yes)__X__ (no)____
If "no," state relationship to policy holder: _____

Date of occurrence: *June 30, 2000*

Date this form completed: *July 6, 2000*

Description of vehicle: *Semi A 1998 Freightliner, cab over engine tractor, Model J, with 18 foot Trailmaster trailer, built for clean hauling. Solid sides and roof.*

Description of occurrence

(Use back of this sheet or additional sheets if necessary.):

On June 30, I was driving my rig on Highway 99 in British Columbia, heading for the northwest end of Garibaldi Provincial Park. I was riding empty to pick up cargo at this ~~expermen~~ experimental stattion just inside the park. I reached the entrance road right about daybreak. The road runs west off the highway and goes straight for about a mile to a gate. I was told it would be open but it was closed and when I stopped I was ~~surr surr~~ surounded by about a hundred or more people, with signs and axes and other wepons. Before the police came they slashed my tires and broke my windsheild and drivers side window.

The reason I had all my repairs done right away was that the next day was a Canadian holiday with nothing open. Also a Friday and then the weekend coming after that. Then Monday was Fourth of July here in the States so there was no chance for repairs unless I did it right away. Besides my contract with the experimental stattion in the park called for delivery to Spokane WA by July 2. And I had a pickup in Spokane to go to Boise ID by yesterday (July 5).

That park, Garibaldi, is out of cell phone range and the land lines were out because of a forest fire so your 800 number was no good. The police told me they had more to do than get into a back and forth with an insurance company so when they offered to radio a tire place in Vancouver I took it. That's why the repairs were done without you getting involved.

Amount of claim (Attach original receipts): $20,082.60

<u>Important.</u> This is for the service call and the ~~insttat~~ installation, and the sixteen tires but only a REGULAR windshield. The repair shop couldn't get the deep tint glass to replace the kind I had. I can get that here in Spokane for $2795 installed. Also, the driver's side window isn't fixed yet. Just taped. They didn't have tint glass for that window either. So this claim above will be for more. For now, the receipts are for $20,082.60.

Eugene R. Packet

ROYAL CANADIAN MOUNTED POLICE
Form 12: Incident Report

Filed by: Constable G.D. Sheaf, Lillooet sub-station
Time of Filing: 1145 hrs. PDT, 00/06/30
Subject: Incident at 'F' Gate, Garibaldi Prov. Park

(See previous reports by this officer and others
regarding the continuing situation at 'F' Gate and
'G' Gate of Garibaldi Provincial Park.)

At or about 0700 hrs. this date, Mr. Eugene Packet, driving
an articulated tractor-trailer, made a right turn into the
'F' Gate entrance road of the park, and drove 1.4 kilometres
to the (closed) gates in front of the Ministry of Natural
Resources Experimental Centre.

According to his statement (verbatim statement on
file, signed and witnessed) Mr. Packet was not aware of the
protest "sit-in" being conducted at 'F' and 'G' entrances to
the park by members of the SOS (Serenity or Sawdust)
environmental activist group. They are objecting to the
possibility that timber-cutting rights may be granted for
this portion of the park. At these same two sites a counter-
protest is being conducted by members of the BFW
(Brotherhood of Forestry Workers), who support the
granting of cutting rights.

Mr. Packet states that as soon as he stopped his vehicle
at the gate, it was immediately set upon and damaged by
members of one or both groups, using stones, axes, and
knives. Mr. Packet remained inside the cab during the entire
incident and was not harmed. There were no passengers.
Our examination of the vehicle confirms that all the tires
were slashed, the tractor's windshield was broken on the
passenger side, and the driver's side window was cracked.
There was no other visible damage.

Customs certification shows that Mr. Packet crossed the

U.S./Canada border with his equipment at Blaine, WA, at approximately 0200 hrs. this date.

Except for an incident on 00/06/22 (see Form 12) at 'G' gate, the protest/counter-protest situation at northwest Garibaldi has been essentially contained for the past month. The two sides have maintained their respective numbers at about fifty and neither has engaged in any aggressive behaviour beyond the daily circle marches. By agreement, both have kept to opposite sides of the entrance road. Neither has attempted to cross the park boundary since the gates were closed (see Form 12: 00/06/04). Statements of witnesses taken by this officer (see following) indicate that this morning's incident occurred because members of SOS and BFW each believed the other was planning to use the truck to disrupt the status quo.

The situation is once again contained.

**From statement of Vern Duffy, BFW
(verbatim statement on file, signed and witnessed):**

"Most of us were still asleep when the truck showed up. Then, as soon as it stopped, one of our guys said he recognized the driver for an SOS type who'd been here before, and somebody else agreed, they'd seen him before, too. So naturally we all got up to stop the vehicle. We figured sure they were going to use that truck to bust the gate. Then just like the last time, a week or so ago, soon as we approached the road, somebody over there on the south side heaved a rock at us and that started it. I guess we were mixing it up pretty good by the time you got here."

**From statement of Shelagh Vaughn-Widmer, SOS
(verbatim statement on file, signed and witnessed):**

"It being just daybreak, there were only a few of us awake but of course the sound of the truck stopping at the gate alerted everyone right away. Then I guess with not being able to see it very well because of the sun in our eyes, and everybody a bit dozy, we must have overreacted.

Thought sure the BFWs were up to something. It was right when the truck stopped that the first rock came at us. Now that the fuss is over, I have to admit the rock was probably aimed at the truck but missed. At the time though, I thought it was intended to keep us back so they could ram the gate."

Reporting Officer's Action:
Charges of Willful Damage (Property) laid against both Mr. Duffy and Ms. Vaughn-Widmer. Neither subject detained.

Gary D. Sheaf, Cast.

? *What is Eugene Packet's attempted, but "pretty clumsy" scam? What in Vern Duffy's and Shelagh Vaughn-Widmer's statements "can't be truthful"?*

FILE # 36

Every Dead Body
Has a Story to Tell

"This body was moved," Sir Avery announced, wrinkling his nose as he peered through rimless glasses at the two policemen on the other side of the narrow examining table.

"Post mortem," he added, thrusting his head forward in a quick chopping motion that told his audience he did not welcome second opinions. Not that either of the two cadet-constables, in their wildest dreams, would have argued with Scotland Yard's chief criminal investigator. He'd been made *Sir* Avery two years before, and there was a story afoot that, during the ceremony, he'd even intimidated Queen Victoria. As it was, both cadets were fully occupied with keeping their insides under control. Moments ago, they'd helped Sir Avery rotate the body onto its stomach. The task was not pleasant.

The murdered man was a Wessex farmer who'd been found at first light by a pair of dairymaids on their way to the morning milking. The back of the man's head had been completely bashed in, and this was the first time either cadet had seen human brains. The fact that sharp slivers of bone punctuated the view, along with some bits of grass, did nothing for their sense of well-being.

"Now, gentlemen, it is important that you do not allow . . ."

Sir Avery had leaned over the corpse with a very large magnifying glass, but now stood up abruptly. "Gentlemen! You can't even *think* of becoming members of the criminal investigation branch, if you won't get close to the crime. Put your noses here!"

Another story told of Sir Avery — one that was easy to believe — was that ever since his knighthood he'd affected an upper class accent that became more pronounced whenever he felt annoyed. *Can't* became a very arch *cawn't* and *branch* turned into a very extended *brawnch*. It always seemed to have the desired effect, though. Within split seconds of "Put your noses here (*he-ah*)!" the cadets had positioned themselves for more optimal learning.

The chief softened ever so slightly. "I appreciate your reluctance, gentlemen. It's not a pleasant sight, but this one's no worse than most. Just the one wound that we can see thus far, but I'd stake my salary there are no others. And, of course, you'd rather not get wet, but . . ." He let the sentence hang.

During the night there had been a torrential downpour. The body was utterly soaked, and little rivulets continued to pour from the dead man's clothes. The top of Sir Avery's shoes were wet now, and it was apparent that he felt the cadets should have the same experience. In addition to creating discomfort for the investigators, the rain had washed away pretty much all the evidence that might have been easily recovered at the scene. On the plus side, however, it had handed some telling facts to the local constabulary who'd first come to the site and then brought the body to Sir Avery. A group of gypsies had been camping at the spot for several days but had left during the night. The depth of the tracks their wagons made in the softened ground made clear that it had been raining for quite some time before they departed. The gypsy group, rightly or wrongly, would have been suspected anyway, just because they were in the neighborhood. But because the body was found near their suddenly abandoned camp — with empty pockets — their guilt had become a foregone conclusion.

"Now, where was I? Yes, examination of the body. Now,

gentlemen, you must not allow yourselves to be misled by drama. The wound, obviously, is a crucial matter to be examined. But you must allow the rest of the body to tell its story too. Every dead body has one to tell. Now, the wound is on the head. That's the case in murders like these more often than not. So a good place to start is the feet. Look. What do those wellies tell you?"

Very self-consciously, both cadets bent over the wellington boots.

One of them spoke. "Wet, like everything else, but not really much mud."

"Aha!" Sir Avery made the two men jump. "Now what does *that* say?"

The same cadet answered. "That maybe he was killed before the rain started? Because . . . er . . . er . . . because otherwise there'd likely be mud on them? But he was found on *grass* in any case. In a cow pasture. Where the gypsies had their camp."

"Indeed!" Sir Avery stood with arms akimbo. It was his approval pose. "Just lock that away for now. Keep going. What else do you see?"

The second cadet pushed in a little closer. Now that the atmosphere was more positive, he didn't want to miss out on the possibilities.

"The trousers are wet too," he offered. "From the rain, of course," he added hastily. "Shirt's soaked too. Rather crumpled. Grass stains on it, especially on the shirt-tail along with quite a bit of — that's blood, isn't it?"

"Quite so!" Sir Avery was sounding triumphant. "More! More! The hands, now. Always look at the hands. What's their story?"

The two cadets competed for the hand on their side of the table.

"Small cut there," the victor said. "On the finger. And another one on the back. They're both healing though. Ah, here's a fairly fresh one. More a puncture than a cut, though. Fingernails are broken. Dirty."

"He's a farmer," Sir Avery said, as if that explained everything. "That was good, gentlemen. Now for the wound. We'll undress him soon and go over the entire body again, but first . . ." Sir Avery leaned over the crushed skull with his large magnifying glass. "Could have been done with a boulder, this blow. Blunt end of an axe more likely. Even a club of some sort. You will note that there is not a great deal of blood remaining in the wound. The most reasonable explanation for that," he continued, "is that much of the blood loss would have taken place where he was killed. That will be the next task: determining just where he was killed."

"But, Sir Avery," the bolder of the two cadets ventured. "Surely he died where he was found. After a blow like that? You . . . you mean he wasn't killed at the gypsy camp?"

"The body was *moved*," Sir Avery asserted. "Post mortem, as I said before. Weren't you paying attention to the story?"

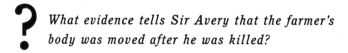 *What evidence tells Sir Avery that the farmer's body was moved after he was killed?*

A Bad Day to
Go up the Mountain

Even on the south face there were still patches of snow on Grace Mountain. Especially in the sheltering roots of trees and in the gullies that opened northward. Higher up, and a few mountains over, some of the resorts were still offering spring skiing, but here on Grace it was obvious now that winter had finally let go. Still, it would be many weeks yet before the first of the season's hikers ventured here.

"I shouldn't be lettin' you go up there," the park ranger had said to Laurie Polk yesterday morning. "Too early." He turned to look out the window and shook his head. "If it ain't snow holdin' you up, it's gonna be mud. No way you should be goin' up."

Laurie hadn't answered. He'd simply stared at the ranger until the officer understood that nothing was going to keep Laurie Polk from going up Grace Mountain to see the death site for himself. The ranger had been right, though. It was tough slogging. The 4 x 4 had been good until the logging road petered out but after that it was footwork. Heavy, grunting, one-determined-step-after-the-other footwork. It had taken Laurie the rest of the day to reach the spot where he stood now, the little clearing where Mindy and Vern had built their emergency shelter. He'd spent the night here on a double ground sheet, wrapped in a sleeping bag, and then, right after sunrise this morning, taken another three hours to get up to Gaston Point to the outcrop that had become Trent and Patti's snowy grave. Laurie looked up at the sun and did a quick calculation. It had taken him two hours to get back down here to the clearing. If he headed out in the next few minutes, he'd make it to the logging road and the 4 x 4 just before dusk. But then what?

"Do I go to the police?" he whispered. Then he shouted in frustration. "Do I accuse my own sister?" A group of jays, startled at this intrusion in their sanctuary, began to scream back at him. Laurie began to yell even louder. "My own sister! I can't believe she had anything to do with this! It couldn't have been her idea. Not Mindy! She's not capable." Laurie held out his hand to a copse of fir trees as though they needed convincing. His voice faded to a whisper again. "Vern. Must have been Vern that . . ."

A single tear rolled down his cheek and he stood there waiting for more but they didn't come. Slowly, Laurie turned and walked a few steps to the edge of the clearing, where Mindy and Vern had hacked down spruce trees to make the crude shelter they said had saved their lives. He put a foot on one of the stumps they'd left, leaned an elbow on his knee and stared at the evergreens. They lay in a tumble on the ground now, their purpose fulfilled. Already the needles were beginning to dry. Not brown or yellow yet, but the summer sun would take care of that soon enough.

"You broke the rules, Mindy." He shook his head. "You and Vern. You broke the rules."

Only after he said it the second time did Laurie realize he was echoing the park ranger. Not the ranger from yesterday morning, but another whom Laurie knew well. They'd been classmates in school, and like everyone else in the little town of Grace Corners, he'd come to Trent and Patti's funeral. At the cemetery, he'd buttonholed Laurie.

"They broke all the rules of common sense, those four." The ranger was gruff and embarrassed, but it was clear he had to get this off his chest. "I mean, three of them grew up here in these mountains. They had to know better. First off, you don't go that high up with snowmobiles. Gaston Point's a good two thousand feet above the highest trail, and it's out of radio range. Sure it's a great spot to go, and you can see for miles, but, still, it's no place for snowmobiles. Especially with a storm watch on."

Laurie had frowned at that. It made the ranger even more agitated.

"Yeah, it was on the radio just like it's supposed to be. Every half hour. 'Storm watch in effect.' You know how it goes. They must have heard it. Had to, but . . . Anyway, 'bout two hours after they left . . . we're guessing two hours . . . that's another thing. I'll tell you about it in a second . . . the storm watch gets upgraded to a storm *warning*! Now, here you go again. That's no big deal, normally. Soon as there's a storm warning, we get on the blower, call everybody in the park and get 'em down and out. But here's the thing. *We don't know they're up there!* Trent and your sister, and Patti and . . . what's Patti's husband's name again? Vern? . . . yeah, Vern! They go up there and they don't tell us!"

They'd been interrupted then. Mindy had asked Laurie to look after Trent's mother. But the ranger's account had stuck with him. Of all the many times since that he'd had to suffer through yet another variation of "How could they have been so foolish?" from one of the locals, it was the pain and anger in the ranger's voice that affected Laurie most. Probably because it reflected his own.

He was not surprised when Mindy told him it was Trent who'd failed to inform the Park Service that they were going up on Grace that day. Trent, Laurie's best buddy since the first grade, the guy that married his sister, the one person who knew all his secrets, was easygoing to a fault. Brilliant and charming but forgetful and utterly careless, he was entirely without ambition, content to turn his back on fabulous SAT scores and a scholarship to work in his uncle's clothing store and become the best snooker player in Grace Corners. As far as Laurie could tell, that hadn't bothered Mindy. She'd been smitten with Trent from the minute she was old enough to tell that boys were different from girls, and the day she finished her nurses training down in Helena, she had scurried home to Grace to marry him. And, as far as Laurie could tell, the marriage seemed to work, in spite of the sharp differences in their personalities. Mindy was active, high-powered, organized. She flung herself at everything she did. Trent coasted.

Interestingly, Mindy's best friend, Patti, was a lot like Trent. Patti had gone off to become a nurse, too. It had taken her a year longer to graduate, what with doing makeup courses and taking a few months off to backpack in Europe. Like Mindy, Patti had come home to Grace. She, however, had brought a husband with her, the only part of the mix that, for Laurie, just didn't fit. To Laurie, Vern didn't seem to belong in Grace Corners. He was too . . . how to describe it . . . too urban, too *Brooks Brothers*. No matter how he tried, Vern always looked just a bit ludicrous in a parka or a John Deere hat.

"Maybe the 'opposites attract' thing is true; the four of them sure seemed to get along." Laurie realized he was talking out loud again when the jays resumed their scolding. The realization made him look up at the sun once more. He sighed heavily, and then, after a final sweeping glance of the clearing and a token kick at the pile of spruce, he began the trek back down the trail.

The four certainly did appear to enjoy one another's company. Granted there weren't all that many young marrieds in Grace Corners, and neither couple had any kids. Still, Mindy and Trent and Patti and Vern carried on as though they were almost glued together. It was not unusual then, that they would go off on a spur of the moment snowmobile run. Well, not *that* spur of the moment, with Mindy involved. She had packed enough lunch for a town meeting, something she always did. And she had seen to it that Trent topped up the gas tanks on both their machines. As for spare V-belts, she had seen to that herself, something Patti and Vern didn't do, as it turned out. Mindy had also put fresh batteries in the CB radio. And, typically, as both she and Vern described to the investigating officers, when the four machines raced single file up Grace Mountain, it was Mindy who was in the lead.

The trouble arose because they decided to run up to Gaston Point to show Vern what Montana looked like from nine thousand feet. Mindy had not heard about the storm watch. She'd been on duty at the hospital until midnight. Too busy to listen to a radio. And because Trent had neglected to get the radio fixed in their 4 x 4, she'd been out of touch. Vern acknowledged quite freely at the investigation that he knew about the storm watch, but pointed out that since coming to Grace Corners he'd found it best to keep his mouth shut on matters that apparently required local expertise to interpret properly.

It was on Gaston where everything went wrong at once. Trent, who'd been feeling queasy ever since lunch, got really sick. Scary sick. It had been tougher getting up than they thought it would be, because the snow was a lot deeper than they'd expected, and more had begun to fall as they arrived. When Trent threw up, and kept doubling over with truly fierce cramps, they knew they had to get back down. Then Patti lost the V-belt on her machine. It broke as she was revving at start-up. Even so, had it not been for the storm, they'd have probably been OK.

Naturally, it was Mindy who took charge. As she had explained it, the snow was too deep to ride double, so it was decided that Patti would stay with Trent. Mindy and Vern would run down to get inside radio range and call the Park Service. If there weren't any hitches, they'd all be home in time for their Saturday night bridge game — assuming that there wasn't something too terribly wrong with Trent. The plan made sense, and, although the blizzard was well developed by the time Mindy and Vern got started, they'd headed down the mountain at breakneck speed.

Everyone in Grace Corners understood completely why the two of them couldn't make it all the way, why they'd had to stop and build a shelter. There was just too much snow. Even the old-timers who hung out at Penski's General Store trading harmless lies admitted the storm was bigger than anything they'd ever experienced. Why, it made the headlines on CNN!

For three days and nights, Mindy and Vern had huddled in their crude shelter, waiting out the blow. It took another day to dig out and work their way down far enough for the CBs to work, and by that time, it was dark. The next afternoon, when the rescue helicopter finally lowered a ranger down into the snow on Gaston Point, he simply signaled to come back up. For Patti and Trent, it was too late.

The 4 x 4 was in sight now, down at the logging road. Laurie looked up and checked the sun one more time. His timing was just as he'd planned. If only the matter of what to do next were as simple.

 Although the four snowmobilers certainly broke the rules of common sense, the chain of events that ended in the deaths of Trent and Patti can be plausibly explained as a combination of carelessness, bad luck, and unfortunate coincidence. Laurie Polk, however, has discovered that one link in the chain did not come about by chance. It was planned. What has Laurie learned that upset him so much?

FILE # **38**

The View from the Parapet

Lying on the roof of Montreal's Duhème Building, his back to the street, it occurred to Percy Winkle that back home in Alsfeldt, Ontario, there was no such animal as a "parapet."

"Come to think of it," he'd said to himself out loud at the time, "there probably isn't a single soul in Alsfeldt with even the foggiest idea what a parapet is." Percy himself had been pretty sure he understood "parapet" when the security guy was telling him and the other sharpshooters where they'd be stationed, but he'd looked it up anyway: "A low protective wall along the roof edge of a building, often ornamental, to offer protection where there is danger of a sudden drop."

Well, the parapet behind him met all the requirements. It was a low, protective wall — came, maybe to his knees when he stood up; it was ornamental — little scoops every couple of feet or so like a phony castle wall; and the Duhème Building was four stories high with a flat roof, so, without a parapet, the odds of someone pitching over the edge onto Sherbrooke Street would be increased considerably.

Percy hunched up onto his elbow and shifted a bit to peer over one of the little scoops. The painter was still there across the street, working on the front of the religious bookstore. Still awful slow and careful, too. Why Teff Schlag, the guy who did everybody's painting back in Alsfeldt, he'd have been finished hours ago.

There was a cop filling up her patrol car at the self-serve gas station. Montreal city cop. Awful small for a cop. She'd taken her hat off and Percy could see her dark skin. East Indian probably, he thought. He wondered what someone her size would do back home when the O'Reilly boys got tight on Saturday night, as they always did, and she'd have to break up the inevitable fight at Bender's Dance Hall.

The two kids in front of the variety store, they were still there. Teenagers. No — older than that. So hard to tell with those wide, sloppy pants, the crotch down at the knees, the plaid shirts hanging open, and the baseball caps on backwards. This was a very ethnic area of the city, and Percy was pretty sure those two were Middle Eastern, Egyptian possibly, or Iranian — maybe Lebanese. He'd had experience with people from the Middle East when he'd done his stint with the UN peacekeeping mission in Cyprus. The families he'd met there, they sure didn't go for the North American slob look. Doesn't take them long to assume all our bad habits, Percy reflected.

The old guy on the corner by the gas station. He was still there on the bench, face held up to the sun. Funny. Percy was sure the guy'd walked in with his cane in his left hand. Now, here it was leaning against the bench on his *right*. Percy tried to focus in a little more. To use the binoculars he'd have to lean over the parapet, and the security guy had said to keep the lowest possible profile for now. Still, that old guy . . . But then, why shouldn't he put the darn cane on whatever side he wanted to? One word Percy did not have to look up was "paranoid." He knew it all too well. It came with the territory.

Movement on the periphery made him start. He stretched to see a little farther. This was a new one. A guy with one, two, three — good God, *five* dogs! Now *that* would sure get attention in Alsfeldt. Just walking your dog — and on a leash, yet — that'd turn heads, but this guy had five! A dogwalker! Somebody that walked dogs for a living! Probably made a good buck, too, from those fancy houses a couple of blocks over. Percy let his body slump back down behind the parapet again, shaking his head at the sheer brainlessness of things that city people do.

He looked at his watch. 1539 hours. A minute left. He could recall perfectly the words of the agent from CSIS, the Canadian Security Intelligence Service. Percy didn't like him. He was kind of smarmy. Superior.

"You make your caution call according to this schedule. Tell us what you see on your section of the route that looks suspicious, and we'll tell you if you have clearance to take anyone down. Has that penetrated? You wait for clearance! This isn't Hollywood! Here are your call times. MacLean, 1538 hours. Winkle, 1540 . . ."

Completely hidden by the parapet now, Percy pulled the tiny microphone closer to make his call. Very soon, a marked man would be walking through his section of Sherbrooke Street. René Sildenafil was head of the anti-terrorism section of the Sûreté du Québec. A CSIS mole planted in an Algerian terrorist cell had learned that Sildenafil was marked for assassination on this stroll, but the man insisted on walking as planned. CSIS had reluctantly agreed, but responded with mass coverage along the route by highly qualified sharpshooters like Percy, brought in from armed forces bases across Canada.

With typical Canadian reserve, however, the CSIS brass had built in a "caution call" element, so that the sharpshooters' skills could be made an absolute last resort. Percy was now about to make his call, and his analysis of anything suspicious.

 Of the five situations that Percy notes, which one does simple logic suggest is improbable, and therefore suspicious?

FILE # **39**

Everything Checked
and Double-Checked

Tony Horrigan stood in the middle of the barn floor, bent slightly forward at the waist, head cocked to the left, hands held out to the side, palms down. He looked like someone ready to flee or jump to safety, but this was Tony's thinking stance. The "double-check" position, his ex-wife used to call it. Accurately, too, for what he was doing at this very moment was mentally running down a list. He would have actually written out the list if he could have — he was that thorough by nature — and checked off each entry with the stubby pencil he always carried in the bib of his overalls. But that was too risky. No point in creating evidence.

Slowly, very slowly, Tony turned a full 360 degrees, careful not to fall through the gap in the barn floor where he'd dropped the lifeless body of Calvin Oates just moments before. Had he done everything? More important, had he done everything *right*?

Looked like it. He turned full circle once more. Behind him was the short piece of plank he'd used on Calvin's head. That would have to disappear, but there was no problem there. He'd take it with him back to his own farm and nail it to the rafters up in the implement shed. No blood on it anyway. Hair either. Cal was bald.

The gap in the barn floor. Tony stepped back a bit, assumed the double-check position again and looked at it carefully. It was definitely wide enough for a man to fall through accidentally. Especially if he was drunk. Typical in many barn structures, it was a hole through which bales of hay could be tossed down to the level below, where the cattle were stabled. Of course, there were no cattle there right now, in the middle of summer, but that was on Tony's mental list, too. Without cattle in the barn, there would be no leftover hay or straw on the floor below. Just nice, solid concrete to greet Cal's head.

Back to the gap. It wasn't *too* wide, was it? Tony had removed a couple of extra boards and stacked them out back with the ones Cal had taken up in the first place. No, not too wide. Typical of Cal, anyway, not to cover up the hole for the summer, when there was no need to toss hay down. Besides, the gap had to be too wide to jump, so the rope story would be more convincing. After dropping Cal's body through, Tony had climbed up to the crossbeam above the gap and tied a piece of rope there. It hung down now to about his waist. An *old* rope, well used. That was on the list, too. Anybody looking at the scene could easily deduce that it was there to get across the gap, Tarzan-like. Again, not unusual in a lot of these old barns. And the possibility that Cal would miss the rope and fall . . . ? Or just simply pitch over the edge? Well, anybody could figure that out. He was well known as a drinker, after all. Besides, he, Tony, would explain the rope business if anybody asked.

Or Edna would, Cal's wife. That was another "x" on the list. They'd agreed, Edna and Tony, that she should be away at her mother's for a couple of days while the event happened. That would not be unusual either. Edna often went there like that. All the neighbors knew it. Especially if Cal went on a bender.

Still another "x": Tony had dropped over last night after chores with some home-made wine and gotten Cal really stinko. Then this morning, he'd shown up again — with the plank — and some hair o' the dog. Whiskey this time. Cal couldn't resist that. As a result the body really smelled of booze. Just to be sure,

Tony had poured a bit on Cal's shirt. Even if there was an autopsy, which Tony really doubted would ever happen, the alcohol would have to show up.

One more circle. The gap, the rope, the plank, the booze . . . check and double-check. Anything forgotten? He peered over the edge. There was just a bit of blood now. Coming from Cal's nose, looked like. Well, that was natural enough. Tony had been careful to drop the body so the head would hit the concrete in roughly the same spot that it met the plank. No, nothing forgotten. Now to go home the back way, along the creek. The same way he'd come this morning. Then he'd get in the old Chev and go over to the Fourth Line and pick up Randy Moses. He and Randy were due to pick up Cal at 11:00 and then meet the others at the mill in town.

Tony Horrigan has set up Cal's death to appear an accident. But an investigating detective with the same double-checking style as Tony might well notice that the scene was indeed set up. What clue might such a thorough detective find?

FILE # **40**

Murder at the CBA!

Wally Barnes allegedly had one good ear but no one at 52 Division had ever seen him use it for telephone calls.

"Say again!" he shouted into the mouthpiece. "C-B-A? What's CBA?"

A pause.

"Booksellers? No kidding! Booksellers have their own convention? And you've got a dead one?"

Another pause. "Yeah, yeah, male, Caucasian . . . gunshots. Look, at 3:00 this afternoon I'm gonna be on vacation. If this is all about books and that, why don't you give it to Ed Noble over in the 55? Isn't his wife a librarian or something?"

During a third pause, Wally hooked the wastebasket closer with his foot and spit into it. "Damned tooth! What's that? No, never mind! Okay. Okay. Metro Convention Centre. I'm on my way."

Twenty minutes later, after losing a screaming match with a transit inspector because he'd parked at a bus stop, and then taking it out on the rookie officer posted at the overnight entrance to the Convention Centre, Wally was standing in the lobby at the foot of an escalator when a uniformed officer approached him.

"Detective Barnes?"

"Yeah, who're you?"

"Indigoni, sir. I'm with 14 Division, but my partner and I caught the 9-1-1."

"Indigoni. That *Eye*-talian?"

"Actually, my grandparents came from Malta, sir. Do you want to go up one floor to the main book display? Victim's up there. Before you talk to the suspect?"

"*Suspect?* Nobody said nothing about a suspect."

"Right after the call went in, detective. Security guard caught him."

"Great! Might be this'll be over and done with in time for — say, is there a garbage can around here or one a' them big ashtrays with sand in it? My tooth . . ."

"There's no smoking here, detective." Indigoni was uncomfortable.

"Don't smoke. It's m' tooth." Wally made a last futile scan for a wastebasket and then took a step toward the escalator. "So, what've you got?" he said.

For the young officer this was easier territory. "The victim is Lawrence Verso. Male, Caucasian. Forty-four. He runs Margins. That's a big book chain. Two shots in the chest. Body's up there in a little café off the display area. Looks like he might have been working in there, making a sign."

"In a café?"

"Seems he was using the coffee maker." The young officer cleared his throat. "Around 3:00 a.m. the security guard hears shots. He's the one who found the body and called 9-1-1. Victim didn't die right away. Tried to write a name on the floor with his finger."

Then, for the first time, P.C. Indigoni revealed himself as the rookie he was. "*Used his own blood!* Got most of the name done, too. J-A-C, something."

Wally swallowed noisily. "Umm . . . that could be Jack or a Jackson. Or one a' those women's names they make outa Jack. Let's go have a look."

He stepped onto the escalator and the younger officer followed.

"Now this security guard," Wally wanted to know, "did he happen to explain what the suspect, not to mention the victim, was doing in a supposedly secure building at three in the . . . Jeez! Where are we? A wind tunnel?"

"The fans, sir." Indigoni replied quickly. "I noticed it earlier. It's even breezier when we get up to the display. Apparently they turn the air conditioning off at midnight and really crank up the ceiling fans. Everything goes back to normal at 7:00 a.m., in a couple of hours."

The older policeman grunted, led the way off the escalator, and immediately began to look for a wastebasket. "Holy Cow!" he blurted at the huge displays. "Look at all those *books*!" He stared in silence, the wastebasket forgotten. "Are there people that *read* that much?" He back-pedaled and peered down a long aisle. "This is as big as a Wal-Mart!"

"Sir? Detective Barnes?" P.C. Indigoni was waving his hand. "Body's this way."

"Yeah, you still didn't tell me what they were doing in here at 3:00 a.m. Jeez, I haven't seen this many books in one place since I was in vice!"

"Yes, sir." Indigoni became very businesslike. "The suspect is Jack Stott. Now, the building goes tight at midnight. All doors on coded entry and video camera, but Stott, he'd have a pass card."

"How come?"

"He's a publisher." The younger policeman replied, as though that explained everything. "Big name in the industry. Owns several companies. He's got a whole row here in the display area. Some of the bigger names have these passes. Verso — the victim — not sure if he had a pass or not. Verso's a chain guy and it's mostly publishers and independents who come to the CBA."

"Independents? Chain guy? How come you know so much about this?"

Indigoni's face turned crimson. "My wife, sir, she's an independent. She has a children's book store."

"A *children's* book store! A store full of books just for kids?"

147

Wally Barnes peered at his rookie colleague in mild surprise. "She make any money doing that?"

"Not yet, sir."

"With all these books, Indigoni, there's gotta be somebody makin' money."

"Yes, sir. Body's right there in the café. I have the suspect secured downstairs. Where we got on the escalator. With the security guard."

Wally nodded and stepped sideways into an open archway. To his right, a scrolling aluminum wall was pulled down to a counter facing the display area. The left wall and the one straight ahead were geared for preparing fast food. The limited floor space was pretty much taken up by the body of the late CEO of Margins, an aerosol paint can, and a handmade poster soaking in a pool of blood. Wally could read DISCOUNT in Day-Glo red. Verso's body lay face up, head toward the arch. "J-A-C" and what was arguably the beginning of a "K" trailed away from bloody fingers on the side nearest the counter.

"'Nough blood to write a whole book, if he'd had the time!" Wally said. "Two entry wounds, looks like. Married, I'd guess, if that ring means anything. Can't hardly see it under all that paint. Indigoni! You make sure somebody tells the wife *before* any media show up. Okay, I've seen enough for now. Let's go see this Stott fella."

"Yes, sir. Back downstairs."

In the security office, Jack Stott was waiting for them. "I'll repeat to you what I said to this . . . this . . . security officer." He didn't wait for Wally to start. "And that's all I'll say until I speak to a lawyer. Yes, I was in the building. I came in at just after midnight; the computer will show that, and the camera. Now, the last time I saw Larry he was up in that little food place on his hands and knees spraying some kind of sign. But he was alive when I left him. I was downstairs in a washroom trying to get some of this confounded red paint off my shoes when this — the guard — came in and, well, *detained* me I suppose you'd say. Now, I want my lawyer."

Wally stared at the traces of Day-Glo red on Stott's shoes and pant cuffs, while idly scratching himself under one arm. He motioned Indigoni into the hallway.

"You take the collar, kid," he said, "I'm going on vacation."

Indigoni peered at Wally Barnes, his face a mixture of confusion and disbelief, until the older man continued.

"Shouldn't be hard to get a confession outa the security guard. It'll look good on your record, too. Better call the forensics weenies, though. And check those door codes and the camera. Don't want to make any mistakes."

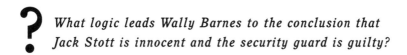

What logic leads Wally Barnes to the conclusion that Jack Stott is innocent and the security guard is guilty?

Solutions

File #1 Blowing Up the Mackenzie Building

? *How does Bruno Plantz know that someone has still been using the Mackenzie Building?*

When Luther Plantz turned on the faucet, the water came out clear. If there was no one using the building, the water from a rusty iron faucet in a building that old would be rusty and dirty for at least the first few seconds, if not longer.

File #2 The Worst Kind of Phone Call

? *What in Allie's story does Karen Tarata not believe?*

Allie told her mother that the girls recognized the boys' car when they saw headlights coming up behind them. In the dark, it's not possible to identify a car when its headlights are shining toward you.

Solutions

File #3   A Courtly Gesture

? *Precisely what did Jerry learn during his courtly gesture?*

When Jerry Fawcett held the woman's hand with both of his, he was feeling for the calluses she would have developed if she had been pushing herself about in a wheelchair. But Jerry, it seems, has discovered that her hands are smooth.

File #4   A Dispute on the Ledge

? *The Stranger and Taas obviously disagree about the height of the entranceway. It should not be difficult to understand what Taas is asking for, but what is The Stranger's reasoning for wanting to top it at its current height?*

Taas is, understandably, opting for comfort. He, and likely most of the adult members of the tribe, will have to stoop inconveniently to get through the entrance. What he has not yet grasped, probably because the concept of dwelling-as-fortress is unfamiliar to him, is the defense value The Stranger is trying to convey. If the villagers can build ladders, so can the raiders from the north. Thus, they may indeed get up to the fortress. But if they have to stoop to get through the entrance, they will be very vulnerable to action from the defenders inside.

File #5   Setting Up the Hit

? *The woman in the conversation above provides a clue as to how she and the man she is speaking to will make sure the victim sits with his back to the door. How will it be done?*

The woman and man speaking on the telephone will arrive at The Lemon Tree before the victim and sit at a table for four near the door. The woman will arrive first, and since it is a restaurant where "nobody takes your coat," she will sit on a chair facing the door and put her coat on another chair. The man will arrive early, choose another chair, and put his coat on hers. (It's about to snow, so everyone will be wearing coats.) The only empty chair will be the one with its back to the door.

File #6   Under the Home Team Bench

? *Since there are only two benches, one on either side of the field, Fritz Lang has a fifty-fifty chance of picking the home team one correctly, but logic should improve the odds considerably. How can he tell which bench is most likely to be the home team's?*

The overwhelming noise of the crowd in support of the tall, thin player strongly suggests that there was a goal or similar achievement by the home team. Only the home team would have enough fans there to make that much noise. Fritz saw the player accept the adulation of the crowd and then go to his bench where, twice more, he had to accept the cheers. Logic suggests Fritz should be looking under this bench.

File #7   First Impressions Revised

? *On what basis does "Miss Brooks" conclude — correctly — that Captain Max Winters did not strangle his wife?*

The situation is arranged to make it appear that Max restrained his wife, Beatty, with his handcuffs and then strangled her before taking his own life. Since, according to Chief Voltz, she was having an affair, there was motive. However, the medical examiner explains that there were no other marks on Beatty except for the ligature marks on her neck. If she had been handcuffed, then strangled, there would have been marks made at least on her wrists as she struggled. "Miss Brooks" correctly concludes that she was strangled first, then the cuffs put on her to implicate

Max. His speculation that a third person may have done this is strengthened by the size of the exit wound on Max's skull. If he was first knocked out with a blow on the head, that evidence could well have disappeared — by design — with an exiting dum-dum bullet.

File #8   Collecting a Betrayal Fee

 What did Sophie do that made Stavros realize she has been here more recently than twenty-four years ago?

When Sophie Andros was in her father's study yesterday, she surveyed the back yard carefully out the bay window and reflected on how it seemed to be smaller than what she remembered. She would certainly have seen the gazebo. As Kimberley says, the gazebo was moved to the other side of the yard a couple of years ago before Constantine's most recent stroke. The "other side," as indicated by the fact that Sophie shades her eyes against the lowering sun to see better, must be to the west, since it is afternoon (Aspen is serving late afternoon tea).

Yesterday Sophie reflected on how, as a child, she would lie in the window seat and watch the birds feeding in the gazebo, with the morning sun in her face. Therefore, the gazebo used to be on the easterly side of the yard. If she has not been in this room for twenty-four years, that is the direction (to the east) she should have looked when told her father was in the gazebo. Instead, she perched sideways on the window seat and looked west.

File #9   Nobody Hides Forever

 Why does Norm Upshur assume that Bovic is left-handed, and why, as Harland Stohl says, does it not apply here?

Norm is assuming that because Bovic was shaving he was looking into a mirror, and that the photo, therefore, is actually a picture of his reflection. In mirrored reflections, images are reversed, so that Bovic, if he is shaving with his left hand, would appear to be shaving with his right. It's a reasonable enough assumption on Norm's part; however, the photograph is a straight-on snapshot, not one in a mirror. Had it been taken in a mirror, the I-H-S would have been S-H-I.

File #10 The Initiation

 Who is the one Veritan, and how did the narrator make his selection?

The last person to speak, the second woman, is the Veritan.

The first woman to speak said she was the Veritan. However, that is the only possible claim she could have made for, if she were a Veritan, she would have said "Veritan," and if, on the other hand, she were a lying Fabrican, she would also have said "Veritan." The same is true for Perry, the only man. His answer, too, could only have been "Veritan." Since the narrator did not hear him, and since the second woman tells the narrator truthfully what Perry said as the waiter dropped the tray, she must be the one Veritan, as she claims to be.

File #11 Taking Over the Thomas Case

 What evidence suggests that Thomas is telling the truth?

The blood that Kirsten finds so difficult to look at indicates that the murder and the theft of the watch took place at different times. When the watch was taken from Velasquez's arm, the scratches did not bleed, which indicates that the body was already dead.

File #12   A Career Adjustment for Lonnie the "Dipper"

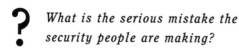 *What is the serious mistake the security people are making?*

If the airline were to place warning signs or posters about pick-pockets at key points, a significant percentage of travelers reading them would instinctively and reflexively touch the pocket or security pouch where they keep their money or credit cards, thereby providing a necessary piece of information for a pick-pocket.

File #13   A Second Witness

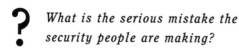 *What is the clue that makes Joy Weng and Sal Forto think Dwayne Bolger is not telling them the truth?*

It is obvious that music is very important to Bolger. His room full of CDs, all arranged on shelves low enough that he can reach them, is where he indulges that passion. The high quality of the equipment also attests to his love of music. But, even with superior equipment, FM bands are sometimes subject to "drift." Bolger says he was in that room all morning and saw the police officers coming down the street to his house. Both Joy Weng and Sal Forto realize that someone with his passion for music would not have been able to tolerate fuzzy radio reception, especially if all it takes to clear it is a slight adjustment of his top-of-the-line equipment. Both officers conclude that he was not in the room all morning as he says. Therefore, he is likely not the witness he claims to be. What they have to dig for now is why he's lying.

File #14   A Preview of the Contract

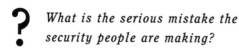 *Within five minutes, Charlotte's claustrophobia is bound to become active and may cause her to be discovered. That's one of the two crisis points. What is the immediate one?*

Charlotte Riston-Winters has just jumped out of the big leather chair where she has been sitting for some time, reading the material on Algernon Methuen's desk. Within seconds, the latter worthy enters the office, goes directly to the chair, and sits. If he is even remotely sensitive to messages from his hindquarters, he will realize that a warm body has recently been in the chair.

File# 15   A Hero Mistreated?

? *What is the "pretty obvious fraud" in*
Harriet (Foster) Blowes's petition?

There are elements of truth in the petition. The Distinguished Service Order (DSO) was established in 1886 and Boer War veterans were decorated with it. The Canadian contingent did distinguish itself at Paardeburg in 1899 and DSOs were awarded after that battle. The Military Cross was established in 1915, around the same time as the Second Battle of Ypres. At this famous gas attack, where the German forces used gas successfully for the first time, the Canadians were the only infantry in the line that did not break and run. However, Harriet Blowes's petition breaks down in the letter from Major Speight. It's dated 1923. No one referred to the Great War of 1914–18 as "World War I" until after World War II had been under way for some time.

File #16   Concentrating the Search

? *How can Willie's body help Vic decide which of*
the two informants is probably the best bet?

The blood from the wound that killed Willie runs from his temple to the back of his shaved head, above his ear. The natural flow, if the car had remained still, would be downward. There had to have been some momentum or force to make it flow backward, a momentum that could only have been achieved if the car was being driven. The second informant is the best bet.

File# 17 Don't Get Caught Speeding in Polk County!

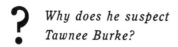 *Why has Eustis Savage become a suspect in the kidnapping (if it is a kidnapping now)? What has Fran picked up that Tony has apparently missed?*

In their perusal of evidence, Fran pointed out two pairs of sunglasses. Eustis Savage emphasized that the alleged officers *looked* like highway patrol officers (i.e., wearing sunglasses) yet his "enhanced powers of concentration" enabled him to offer the "brown eyes" of one of them as part of his description. Not possible in a few seconds if the eyes are behind sunglasses, and kidnappers as savvy as these have been surely would not have taken off sunglasses and given away an identifying feature. Eustis (and quite possibly Chabot) is part of a setup.

File #18 The Unseen Hijacker

Why does he suspect Tawnee Burke?

When the plane was searched after the incident, nothing was found, so either the dynamite was tossed out or there never was any. If unstable dynamite had been tossed out between Tucson and Phoenix, or if the hijacker had jumped with it (at great risk), there would have been a noticeable explosion on contact with the ground, but a search of the area beneath the radar-tracked flight turned up nothing. The only possible conclusion, then, is that there never was any unstable dynamite. That suggests two possibilities: that there may never have been a hijacker, and Tawnee Burke, therefore, has the $250,000; or, that if there was one, and he has parachuted with the money, he is in cahoots with Tawnee Burke. At the very least, she should be investigated.

File #19   A Rash of Break-ins

 Why does Ed Stock suspect that P.C. Johnson may not be a P.C. (police constable) at all, and that their house was being "cased"?

Only in emergencies (and in movies) do police officers who are on duty drive into long driveways. Properly trained officers back in, so that it is harder to box in their car and so that, if they are suddenly called away, they can exit more quickly. "P.C. Johnson" drove into the Stock driveway. He also gained vital information about the layout of the house and about its relative lack of security.

File #20   Random Shots by the River

What is Tim going to do with it?

He is going to sniff it. The Greevelys, apparently, are more than a little accustomed to police visits and questions, so the woman who answered the door may have anticipated Tim's questioning by putting Lawson in front of the TV at the time the shots were fired down at the river flat. If he was indeed watching TV and not part of the campfire shooting group, his shirt will contain normal farm and body odors. If, however, he was part of the group, the shirt, especially a heavy woolen plaid shirt, will smell of easily identifiable wood smoke.

There is a very slight chance that Lawson, if he went out last night, did not wear the shirt, but that is slight. The shirts are "standard"; it is still spring and therefore cool enough, especially in the evening and at night.

File #21 An Eye for Details

? *In the crime scene that Breen Morris is investigating, what is the detail that doesn't fit?*

Breen notes the beads of condensation on the label of the champagne bottle, something that happens when a chilled bottle of liquid is exposed to room temperature. What bothers her, and what she has to investigate, is that the champagne appears to have been placed in this bucket much closer to the present time, 8:10, than at a time before 5:00 p.m., when the victim was supposedly finishing a drink with a client. By now, the beads of condensation would have evaporated as the champagne bottle's contents gradually rose to the same temperature as that of the room.

File #22 Nathan Greeley's Personal Effects

? *Something in Nathan Greeley's personal effects has made Sergeant Shelley Budgell suspicious of his alibi. What is that, and why does she think he may have been in Denver, after all, at the time of the shooting?*

The Movado watch. It is set two hours behind the time in Detroit, where Greeley lives. Regardless of whether Shelley knows that Denver is in the Mountain time zone, two hours behind Detroit, which lies in the Eastern time zone, she will at least know that the two cities are in different zones. It is extremely unlikely that Greeley would reset his watch from Detroit's time to Denver's if he was there for less than twenty-four hours. Shelley feels it is possible that he was in Denver for a longer time than that and that someone, an accomplice, may have used Greeley's ticket on Flight 328 to give him an alibi. If that can be established, it may help prove that Greeley was in Denver at the time of the shooting and took a later flight to Detroit.

File #23 Hunting the Blue Morpho

? *What makes Judy Larabee's father think*
Gustavo is not what he claims to be?

When travelling on foot in jungle, bush, rainforest, or any kind of dense undergrowth, people with even a tiny amount of experience never walk "tight behind" someone else. In fact, the practice is to consciously walk several paces or more behind a person in front of you to avoid whipping branches. In areas where there is no established trail, it's even more important because of unseen holes, soft surfaces, etc. If the first person goes in, the second can stop, and then be able to help the accident victim.

File #24 All the Pieces in Place

? *Morry Green has put all the pieces in*
place for a perfect murder. Except one.
What one mistake has he made?

Morry put masking tape on the window to show where the "murderer" broke into the house. By doing that, he left his fingerprints on the one item where they would not be naturally found.

File #25 The Kid's Idea

? *In "the kid's" scene, the Contessa*
manages to poison the cardinal. How?

There was poison on one side of the knife blade, the side against the portion of apple the cardinal ate.

File #26 The Case of the Skull & Anchor

? *How did Louis Raines-Prideau*
"figure that"?

After Louis sought "Horse" Kahane's OK to cut the fishing line free from the skull, he took a long, narrow pair of scissors and carefully wedged one blade between the line and the bone. The line was tied tightly to the bone, therefore, so there could not have been any flesh on the skull when the line was put on.

File #27 Milverton's Deception

? *Birdwell is exasperated because he realizes that Milverton*
must be engaging in a fraudulent deal with the printer.
What is the deception?

Neither book has pages that need to be repaired (except for perhaps the title page of one and the end page of the other). If George Eliot's (Marian Evans's) *Middlemarch* stands in "proper alphabetical order" to the left of *The Mill on the Floss*, and the "burrowing creature" has eaten its way from the title page of the former to the end page of the latter, then it ate only through the front cover of *Middlemarch* and the back cover of *"Mill."* The pages will be undamaged.

File #28 Fishing out of Season

? *What is the date of the first trip out? And what are the*
three fish-and-game law violations on this first trip?
Who committed them?

On the first trip out (April 22) Gabriel Long took trout, Fabian March took whitefish, and Francis Cadeux, bass. (Hester took pike, legally.) Since the trout and whitefish seasons did not open until April 29, and the bass season did not open until April 23, the three broke fish-and-game laws.

The assistant warden made a separate note each time he followed the four suspects. Since there were four sheets, he made four surveillance trips. The fourth was on May 6 ("dated a week ago"). Trip three was on May 3; trip two on April 29, and trip one on April 22 (a week before Hester's "whitefish trip").

From the notes, Chief Warden Smith knows who caught what on certain of the trips (see below in upper case). Because on each trip each person caught a different species, and a different one each time, the Chief needs only to fill in the blanks logically to determine who caught what on April 22.

	April 22	April 29	May 3	May 6
Gabriel Long	trout	BASS	whitefish	pike
Fabian March	whitefish	trout	PIKE	bass
Hester Long	pike	WHITEFISH	bass	TROUT
Francis Cadeux	bass	pike	TROUT	WHITEFISH

File #29 The Last Wish of Latimer Orkin

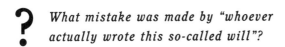 *What mistake was made by "whoever actually wrote this so-called will"?*

When Doctor Tranh handed Nona the mechanical pencil and asked her to write something, so that the results on paper could be compared with the "will," he twisted the lead up out of the pencil. If Orkin had used it *in extremis* to write his new final will and then died during the process, more lead would not have to be twisted up for the pencil to be used the next time. There would still be lead there. (If the lead had merely broken, when Nona first used it there would have been graphite splatters from the jagged edge of the break, so the marks on the paper would not have been "exactly the same.") The writer (Misty Duvall, perhaps?) must have automatically retracted the lead after writing.

File #30 Death in Benton County

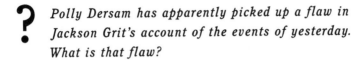

Polly Dersam has apparently picked up a flaw in Jackson Grit's account of the events of yesterday. What is that flaw?

According to Jackson Grit, he saw his deaf son react at the sudden appearance of a shadow while probing with a stick into the pool. The implication is that Jerome then swung out of a perceived need to defend himself. The flaw in Jackson's account is the shadow. Polly had backed her cruiser to the site and was leaning on the back of it to hold her face to the late afternoon sun. Since the incident happened "yestiddy" in this place at about this same time, there would be no shadow cast over the pool, nor over anyone squatted at the pool. Any shadows would be cast the other way, away from the pool.

File #31 The Coroner's Decision

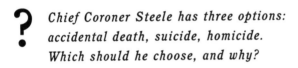

Chief Coroner Steele has three options: accidental death, suicide, homicide. Which should he choose, and why?

Homicide. The telling clue is the distance the body on the sidewalk lies from the building's wall. An object heavier than air will fall straight down unless it is propelled by some means. If Ms. Avia Lund-March fell from the balcony she would have landed closer to the building. Had she made a "standing long jump" into the air in a suicide attempt and then fallen straight down, the body would also have been closer. (The record for standing long jump at the Olympics is 11 feet (3.4 m); it is a record in men's. It was never included in women's track and field and has been discontinued in men's.) Only the propulsion of being thrown off the balcony could achieve that distance.

File #32 Where to Send the Dogs

 Why is Michael de Sousa so sure the kids went that way and not along the fork to the left?

Michael used elementary physics. When he knelt on the left fork to listen for the sound of water coming over the Step One dam, he pushed his fingers into a ridgeline of dead pine needles and maple keys that ran along the middle of the path. The time is late autumn, almost winter, so many of these would have fallen to the ground by now and onto the surface of the lake. Because of the heavy rainfall over the past several days, a high level of water had been pouring over Step One, and the level of Middle Lake, naturally, would have risen. The force of water from Step One would cause a mild current toward the shores of the lake and the needles and keys would naturally float to the edge. When the flow from Step One was shut down, and the flow over Step Two increased, the level of water in Middle Lake would go down quickly, leaving the ridge of needles and keys behind. Michael has deduced that the left path has been under water, so the kids would have gone to the right.

File #33 Time for the Mortars?

 Why does Sergei believe that the Thracian is concocting something?

The day is hot, and so windless that the cloud of dust raised by the Thracian on his horse does not move. That being the case, a flag carried by slow-moving infantry would not wave either, at least not enough to be seen. The Thracian, therefore, would not have been able to distinguish the flag of France. (During the Crimean War (1854–1856) the French tricolor was, as it is today, three vertical bars: red, white, and blue. The Imperial Russian flag, until the Russian Revolution in 1917, was three horizontal bars: white, blue, and red.)

File #34   When Bad Things Come in Threes

 What did Moira Nairn discover during her visit to the backyard that now leads her to believe there may have been "some tampering" in at least one of the three incidents at Happy Sunbeam Nursery School?

Moira picked up a large bolt from the refuse. Its size indicates that it could only have come from the Kindergym and that it was important to the integrity of the structure. The head had a light coating of rust, which is normal because of oxidation. The head would be exposed to air. She ran her fingers along the length of the thread (which indicates that the nut is missing), and then immediately after, put her hands on her knees. When she came into the light, she noticed a grease mark on her knee, which must have come from the thread part of the bolt. This shows that the nut had been removed from the bolt recently and in a single action. If the nut had come loose gradually over time and fallen off, the oxidation process that developed normally on the head of the bolt would have occurred along the thread too, and Moira would not have gotten grease on her finger when she touched the bolt. It appears that someone removed the nut so that activity on the Kindergym would cause this key bolt to fall out.

File #35   Incident at Garibaldi Park

 What is Eugene Packet's attempted, but "pretty clumsy" scam? What in Vern Duffy's and Shelagh Vaughn-Widmer's statements "can't be true"?

Constable Sheaf's report makes clear that all the tires on Packet's tractor-trailer were slashed, yet Packet is claiming replacement costs for sixteen tires. No "semi" combination (a.k.a. tractor-trailer) has sixteen wheels. Semis have two wheels on the very front axle (one at each end); all other axles have "duals" (two at each end). Thus, a typical "semi" has ten wheels in total, or fourteen, or eighteen, and so on, depending on the number of axles. The number goes up by *four* with each increase in size. Easy to check the next time you are on the highway.

Eugene lost all his tires in the incident. It's a safe bet he's not claiming for fewer tires than were slashed, so he doesn't have an eighteen-wheeler. He must be trying to scam extra tires out of the Access Claims Department.

Duffy and/or Vaughn-Widmer may be lying about who threw the first rock, not to mention where the rock in question was aimed. And given the likelihood of sympathetic witnesses on both sides, it's easy to understand why Morris Freeman doubts the charges against them will hold up. In their statements, however, both have lied to Constable Sheaf.

Vaughn-Widmer said that her side was confused by the sun in their eyes. Yet the time was daybreak; the truck was facing west, and the SOS group was on the south side of the road. That means they were facing north. Not exactly into the rising sun!

Duffy claimed that two of his people recognized the truck driver. However, the BFW group was on the north, or passenger side, of the truck. At the time, the sun was at horizon level, behind the truck, putting the cab and its tinted windows in shadow. They probably didn't even see the driver, let alone recognize him.

In Freeman's opinion, a legal challenge of their statements could recover some of the claim costs.

File #36 Every Dead Body Has a Story to Tell

 What evidence tells Sir Avery that the farmer's body was moved after he was killed?

The farmer's body was dragged by the feet, and face up, to the site of the gypsy camp. The principal clue is on the shirt and shirt-tail. As the body was dragged along the grass (hence the grass stains and bits of grass in the wound), the shirt, and most especially the tail of the shirt, gradually crumpled up at the top of the torso, came in contact with the wound in the skull, and thus acquired bloodstains. On grass, especially on wet grass, the body would have slid along quite easily.

During, before, and unfortunately, even since Victorian times, nomadic gypsy groups have often been blamed for local crimes. While Sir Avery has not eliminated them as suspects, he realizes that a murderer would use their presence as an opportunity to put suspicion on them if possible.

File #37 A Bad Day to Go up the Mountain

? *Although the four snowmobilers certainly broke the rules of common sense, the chain of events that ended in the deaths of Trent and Patti can be plausibly explained as a combination of carelessness, bad luck, and unfortunate coincidence. Laurie Polk, however, has discovered that one link in the chain did not come about by chance. It was planned. What has Laurie learned that upset him so much?*

According to Mindy and Vern's account, once the snow was too deep and heavy to go any farther in their race down the mountain, they had hacked down spruce trees for an emergency shelter. Yet the stumps are short enough for Laurie to easily lift a foot and rest it on one of them. This means the trees had to have been cut (and likely the shelter built) *before* all the snow fell. Mindy and Vern had *planned* to stop where they did and wait for the storm they knew was coming. Laurie's reluctant discovery shows that carelessness, bad luck, and unfortunate coincidence had very little part to play in the deaths of Trent and Patti.

File #38 The View from the Parapet

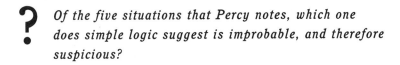 *Of the five situations that Percy notes, which one does simple logic suggest is improbable, and therefore suspicious?*

The slow painter merits attention, but his pace is not necessarily unusual among tradespeople. Dogwalkers are common in most North American cities when there are residential areas nearby. The young men of Middle East background would draw attention because the threat is from an Algerian cell, but nothing suggests that they are doing anything wrong. The old man is no more suspicious than any of the others. Only the police officer is doing something odd. In cities, patrol cars are gassed up at central depots, usually where the cars are kept and maintained. For her to fill up at a commercial gas station is neither typical nor logical.

File #39 Everything Checked and Double-Checked

Tony Horrigan has set up Cal's death to appear an accident. But an investigating detective with the same double-checking style as Tony might well notice that the scene was indeed set up. What clue might such a thorough detective find?

A careful investigating detective who checks every aspect of the scene would certainly crawl up to the crossbeam where Tony tied the rope that Cal supposedly uses to swing across the gap. If Cal had been using the rope on a regular basis, there would be evidence of that use worn into the crossbeam.

File #40 Murder at the CBA!

? *What logic leads Wally Barnes to the conclusion that Jack Stott is innocent and the security guard is guilty?*

The video camera and the computer-code entry system to the building will confirm whether Jack Stott came in when he says he did. It will also show whether anyone else came into the building. Unless someone did, only Stott, Verso, and the guard were inside at the time of the murder.

Stott says he talked to Verso while the latter was painting the sign or poster. That is true because Stott has paint on his shoes and cuffs. This, no doubt, is the result of the wind created by the fans. Therefore, Stott was indeed present while Verso was painting. Stott would then have seen Verso painting with his *left* hand. (The ring finger is almost obscured by paint.) However, the writing of J-A-C is done near Verso's right hand, something Verso plainly didn't do himself, and which Stott, if he were the shooter in what is clearly a premeditated murder, would not have done. The only other possibility then is that the writing of J-A-C and the shooting were done by someone else in the building, and if the security guard was the only other person . . .